More MOVIE HITS FOR THE TEEN PLAYER

EASY PIANO ARRANGEMENTS BY DAN COATES

CONTENTS

BELIEVER
BE COOL 2

CORPSE BRIDE (MAIN TITLE)
CORPSE BRIDE 5

THE BATMAN THEME
BATMAN (THE MOVIE) 8

BREAKAWAY
PRINCESS DIARIES II 12

THE CHAMBER OF SECRETS
HARRY POTTER AND THE CHAMBER OF SECRETS 16

DOUBLE TROUBLE
HARRY POTTER AND THE PRISONER OF AZKABAN 20

EVERYTHING BURNS
FANTASTIC 4 24

FOR YOU I WILL
SPACE JAM 29

HOW DO I LIVE
CON AIR 32

MUSIC OF MY HEART
MUSIC OF THE HEART 35

HOGWARTS' HYMN
HARRY POTTER AND THE GOBLET OF FIRE™ 38

I BELIEVE IN YOU AND ME
THE PREACHER'S WIFE 40

INTO THE WEST
LORD OF THE RINGS: THE RETURN OF THE KING 44

MAGIC WORKS
HARRY POTTER AND THE GOBLET OF FIRE™ 50

THE NOTEBOOK (MAIN TITLE)
THE NOTEBOOK 62

STAYIN' ALIVE
SATURDAY NIGHT FEVER 54

TAKE MY BREATH AWAY
TOP GUN 58

DAN COATES® is a registered trademark of Alfred Publishing Co., Inc.

© MMVI ALFRED PUBLISHING CO., INC.
All Rights Reserved   Printed in USA

BELIEVER

Words and Music by will.i.am and John Legend
Arranged by Dan Coates

4

CORPSE BRIDE
(Main Title)

Music by Danny Elfman
Arranged by Dan Coates

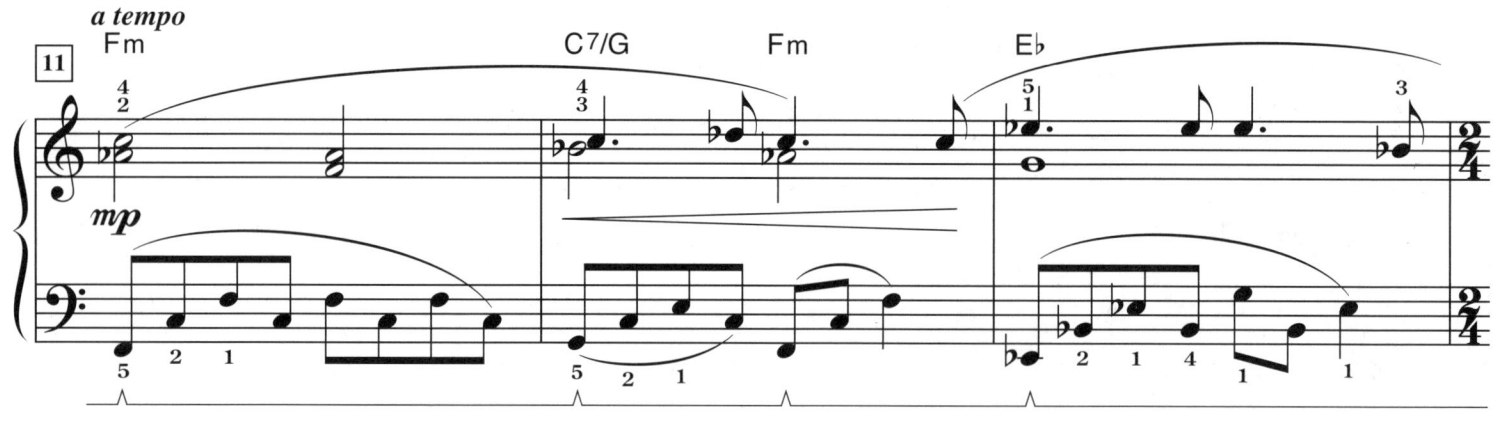

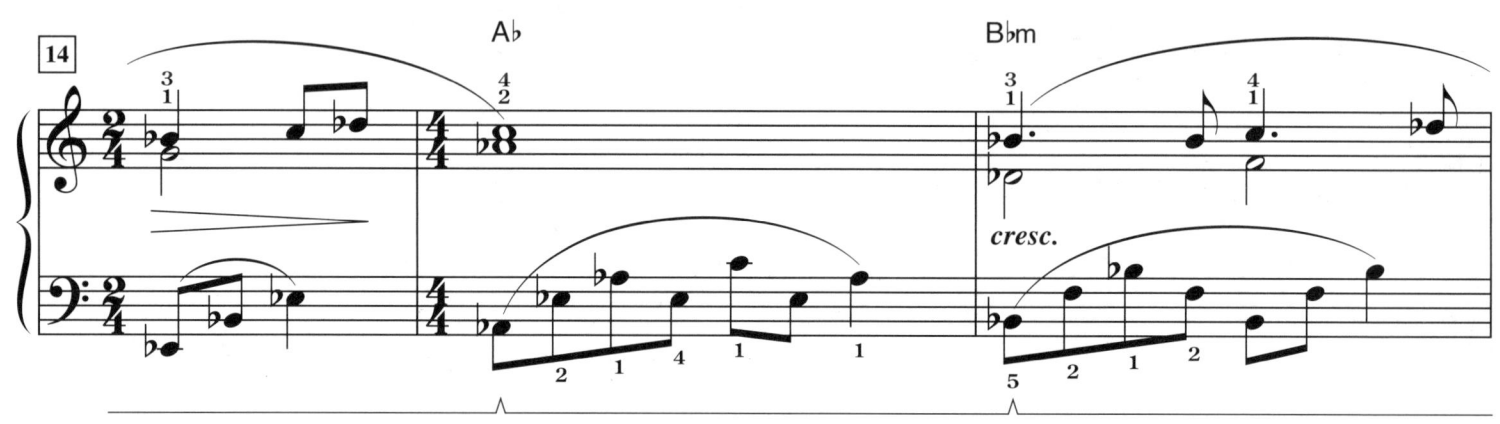

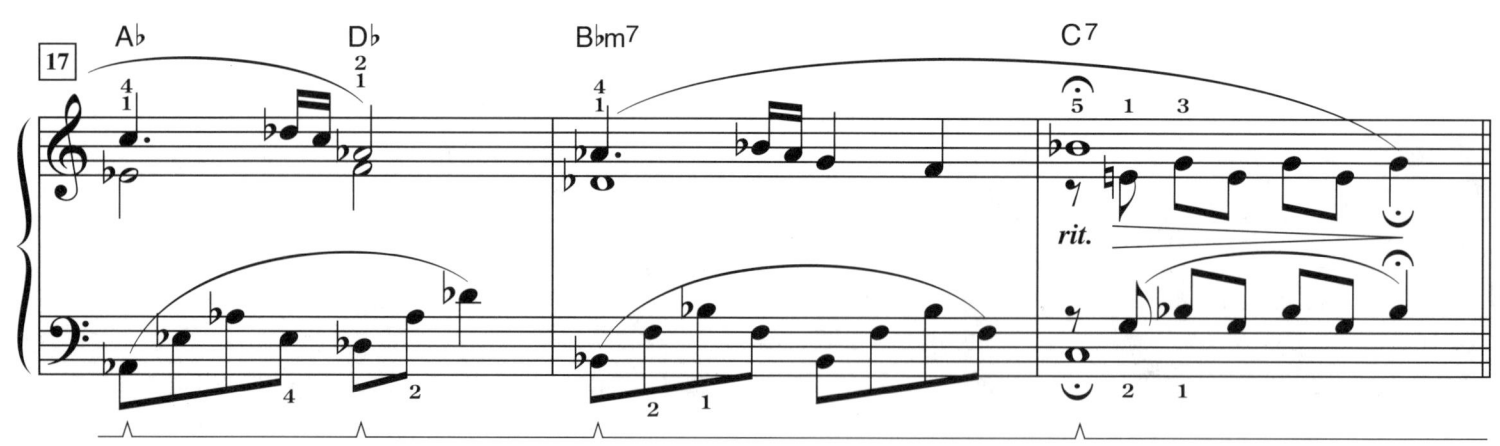

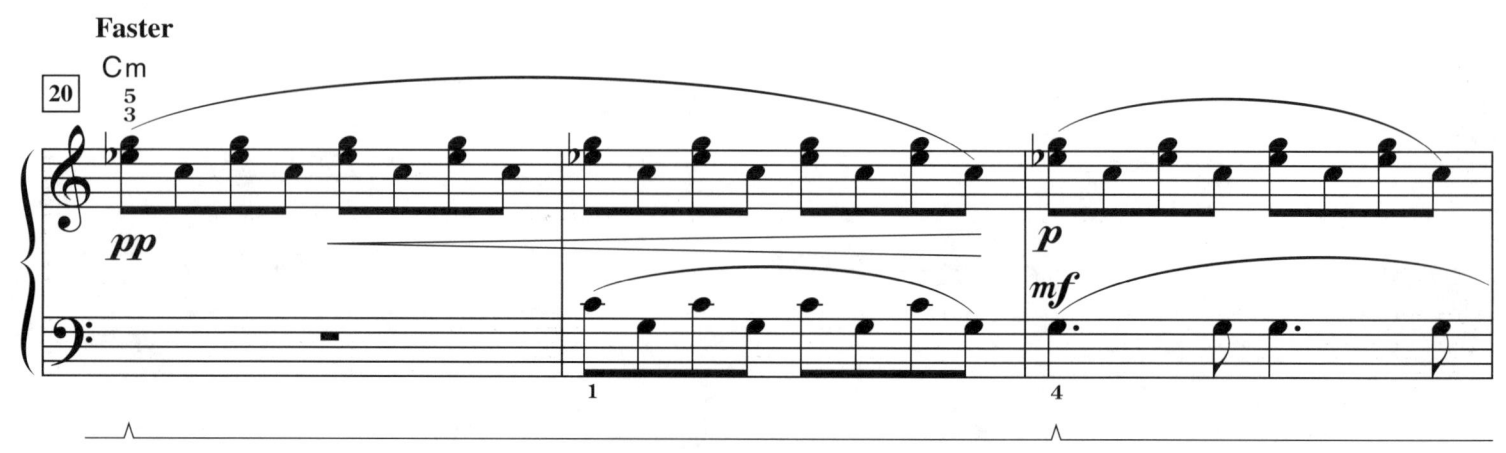

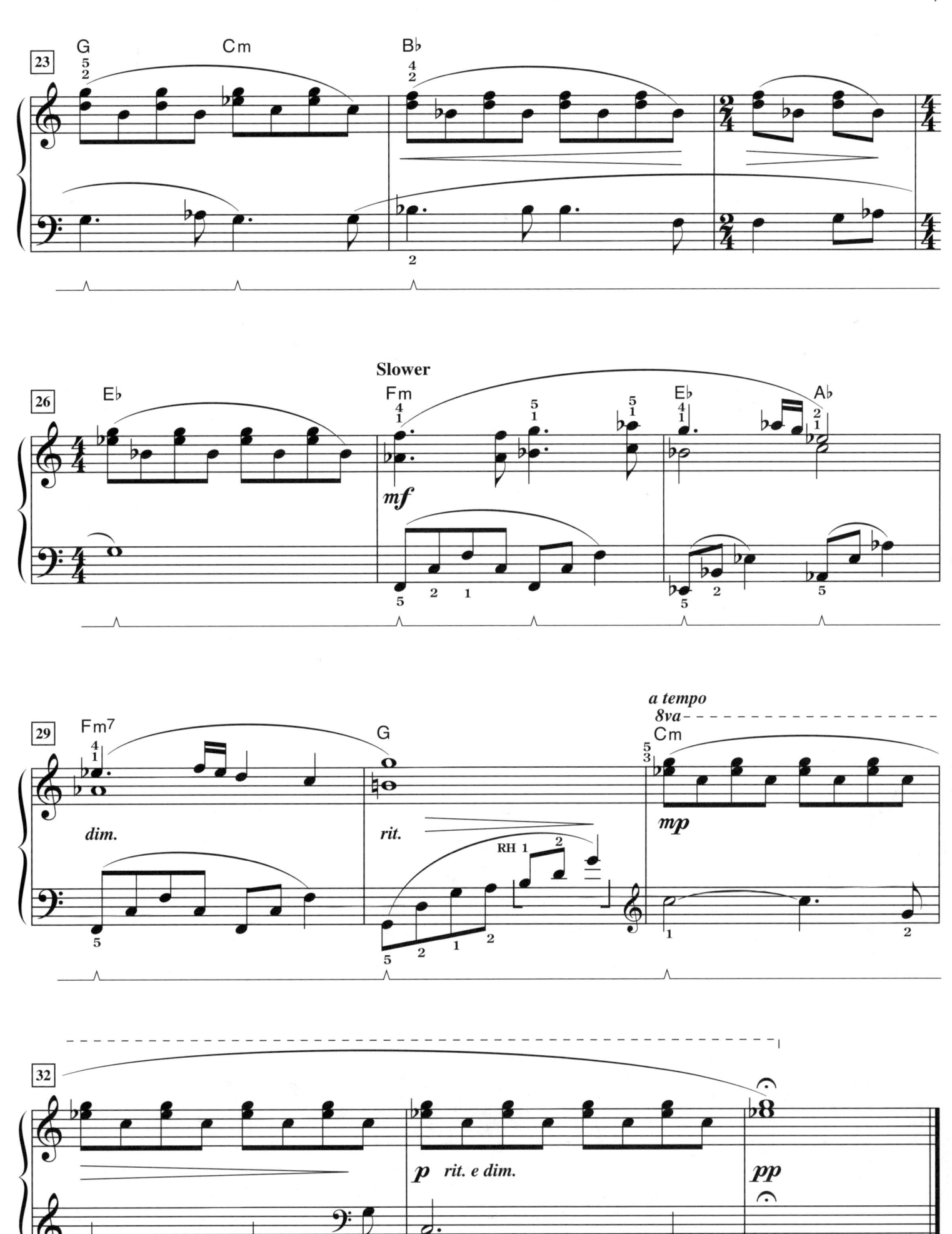

THE BATMAN THEME

By Danny Elfman
Arranged by Dan Coates

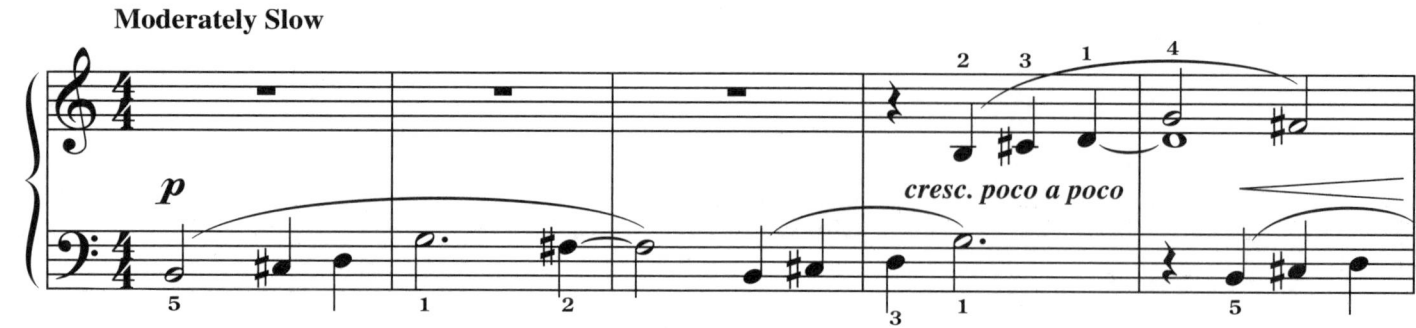

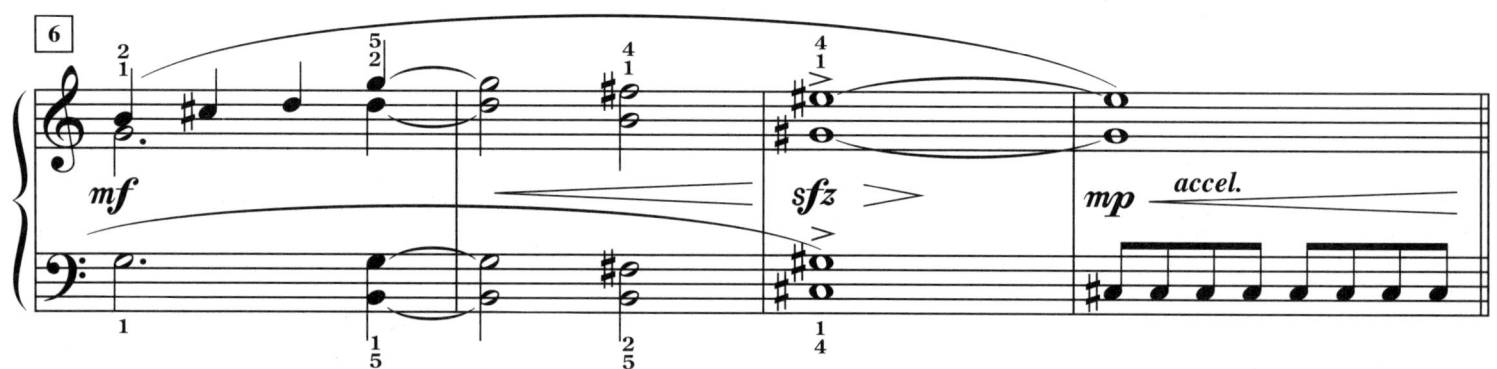

BREAKAWAY

Words and Music by Matthew Gerrard,
Bridget Benenate and Avril Lavigne
Arranged by Dan Coates

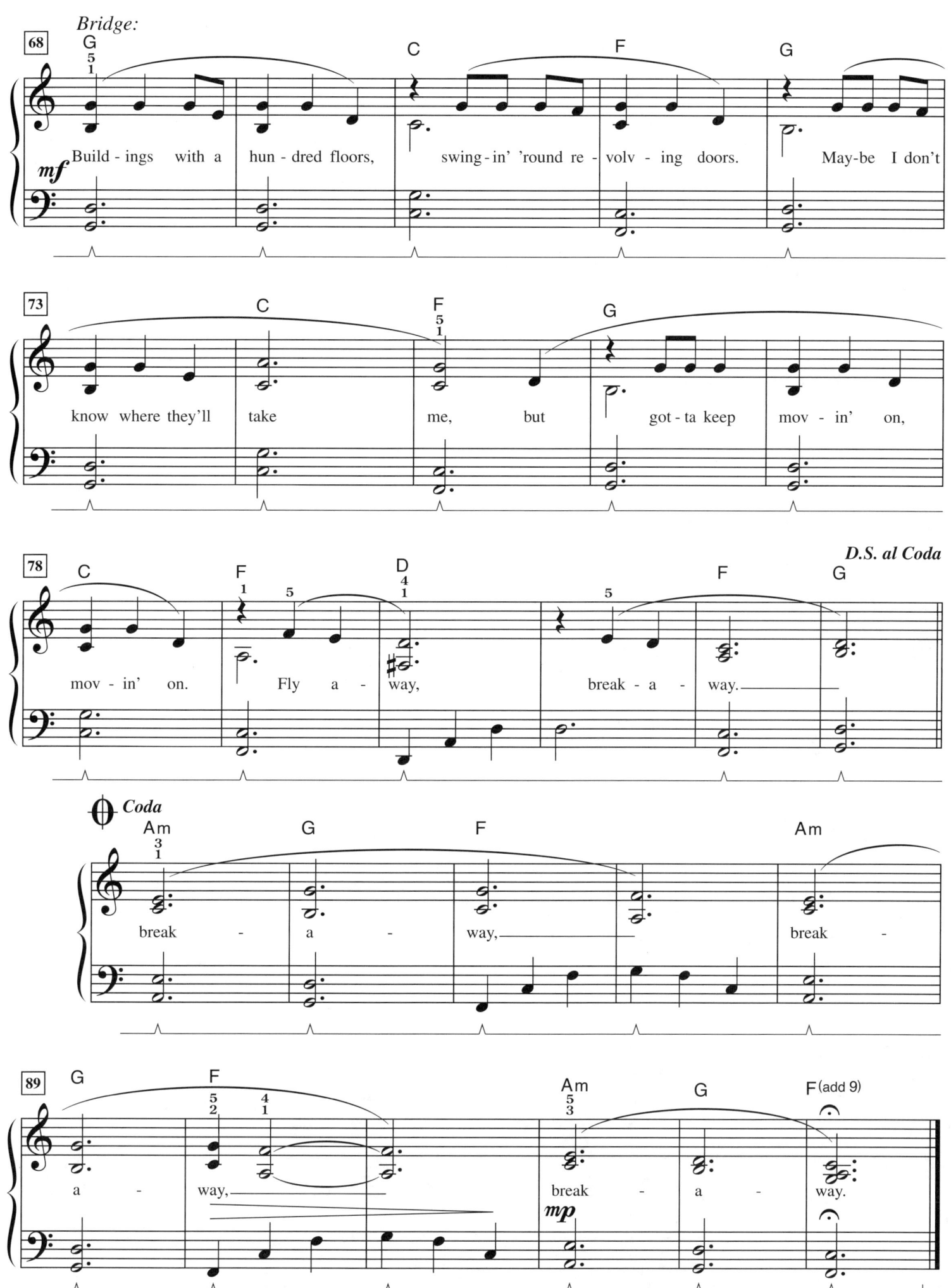

THE CHAMBER OF SECRETS

Music by **JOHN WILLIAMS**
Arranged by Dan Coates

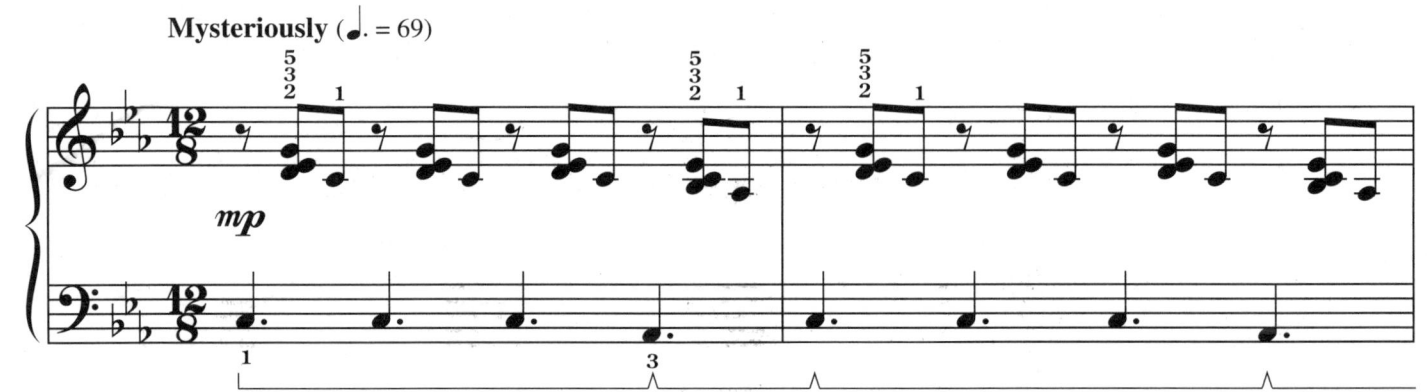

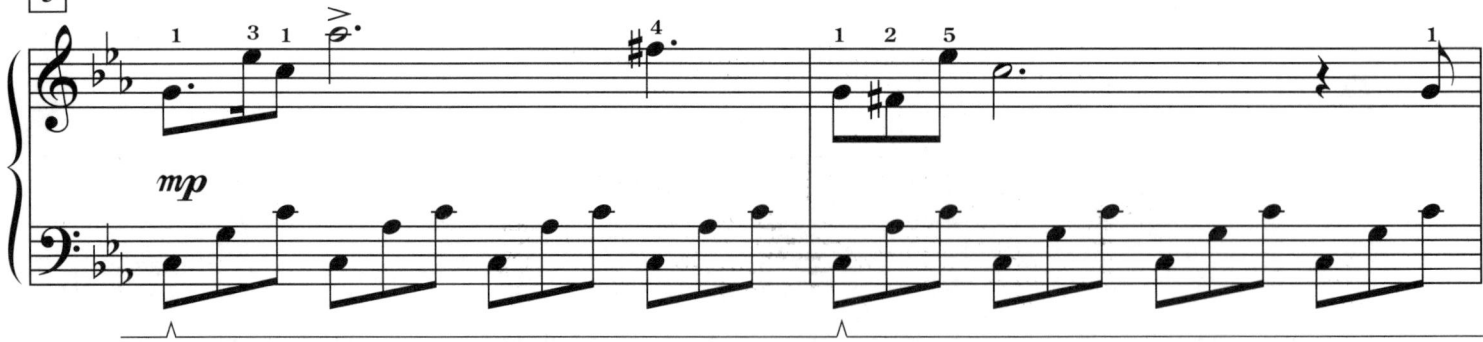

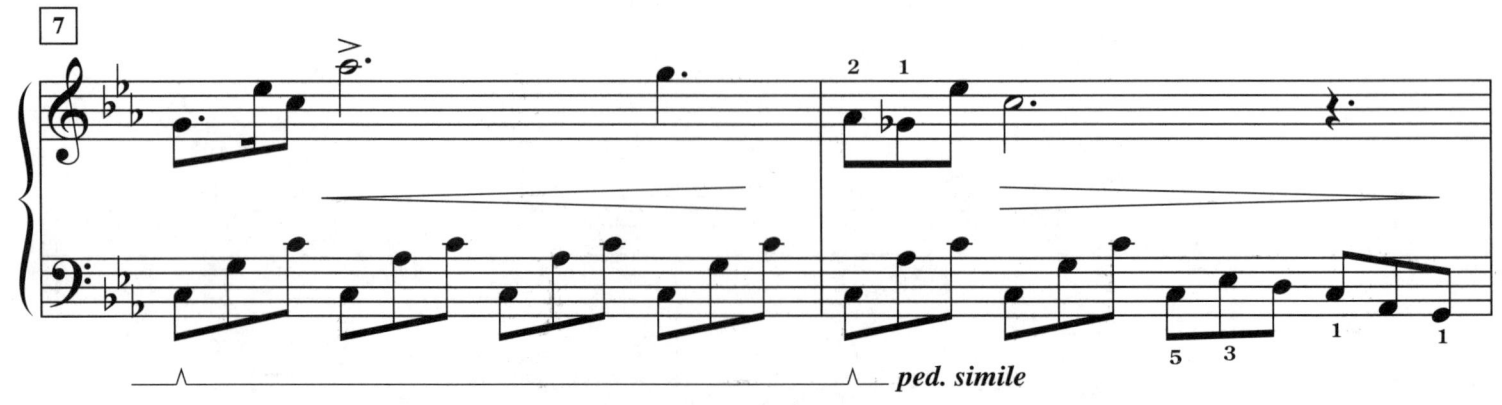

DOUBLE TROUBLE

Music by **JOHN WILLIAMS**
Arranged by Dan Coates

Spirited ($\quad = 92$)

Dou - ble, dou - ble toil and trou - ble; fire —— burn and caul - dron bub - ble.

Dou - ble, dou - ble toil and trou - ble; some - thing wick - ed this way comes!

Eye of newt and toe of

frog,   wool   of bat and tongue of   dog.   Ad - der's fork and blind-worm's

cresc.

sting,   liz - ard's leg and owl - et's   wing.

f

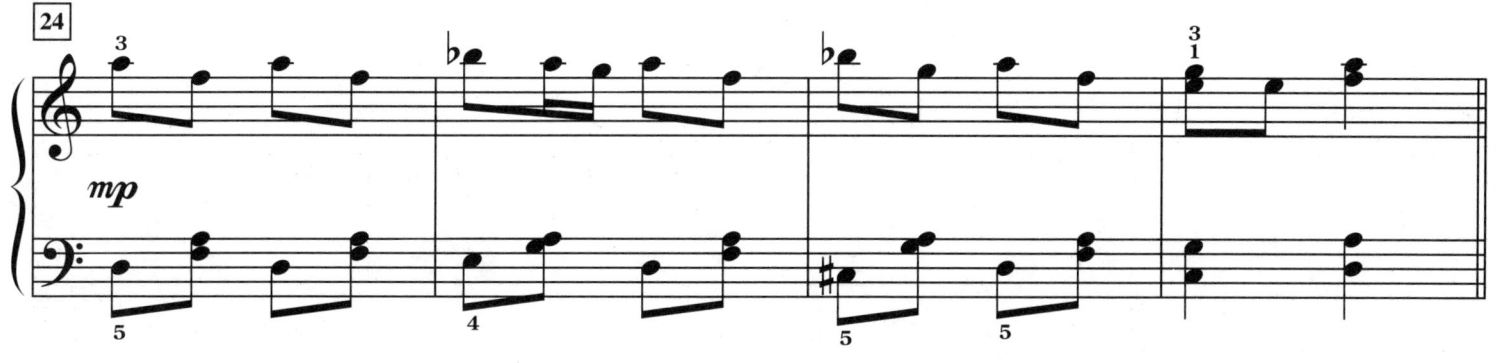

mp

Dou - ble,   dou - ble   toil and trou - ble;   fire——— burn and   caul - dron bub - ble.

mf

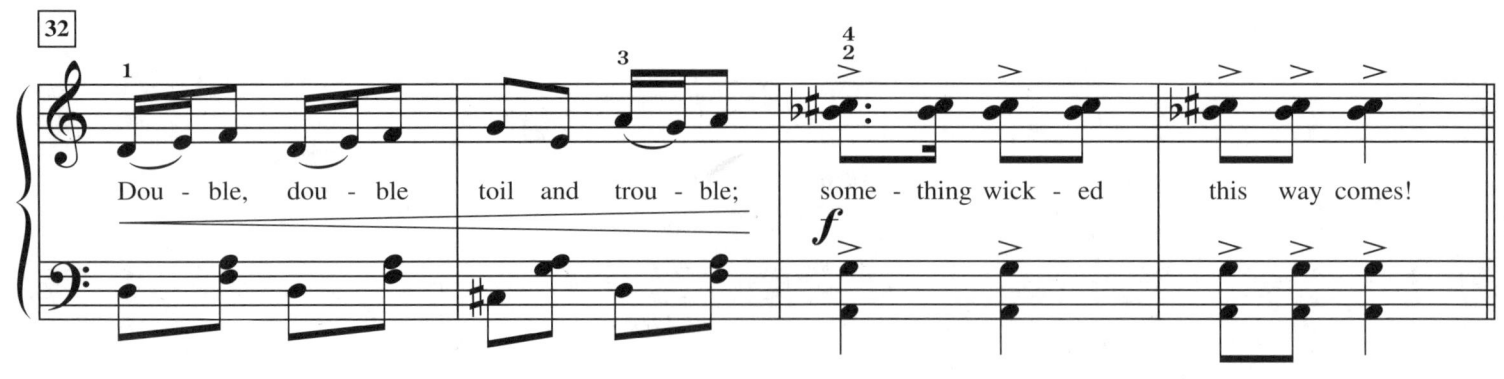

Dou - ble, dou - ble toil and trou - ble; some - thing wick - ed this way comes!

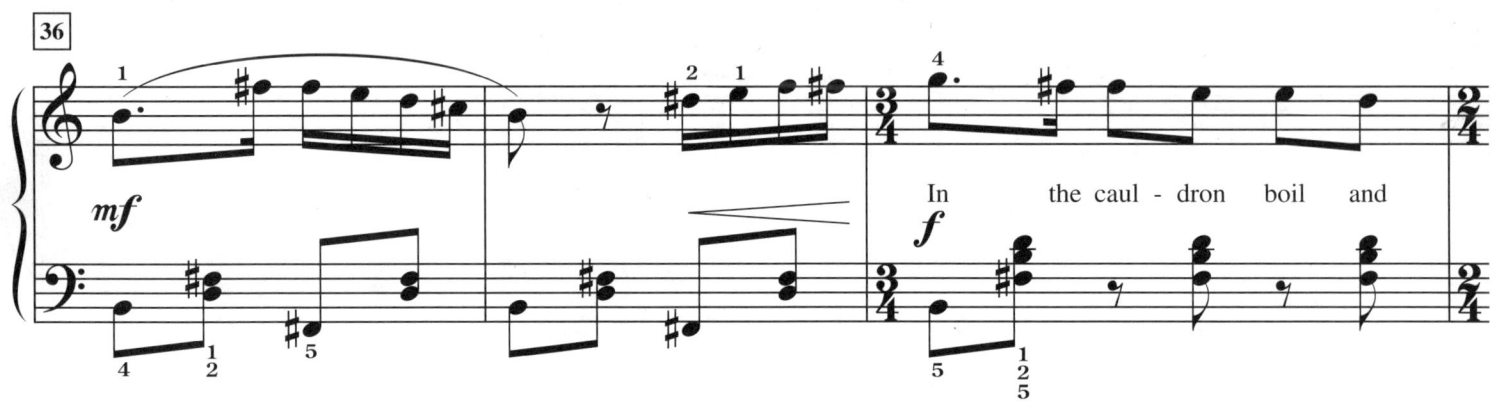

In the caul - dron boil and

bake, fil - let of a fen - ny snake.

Scale of drag - on, tooth of wolf, witch - es' mum - my, maw and

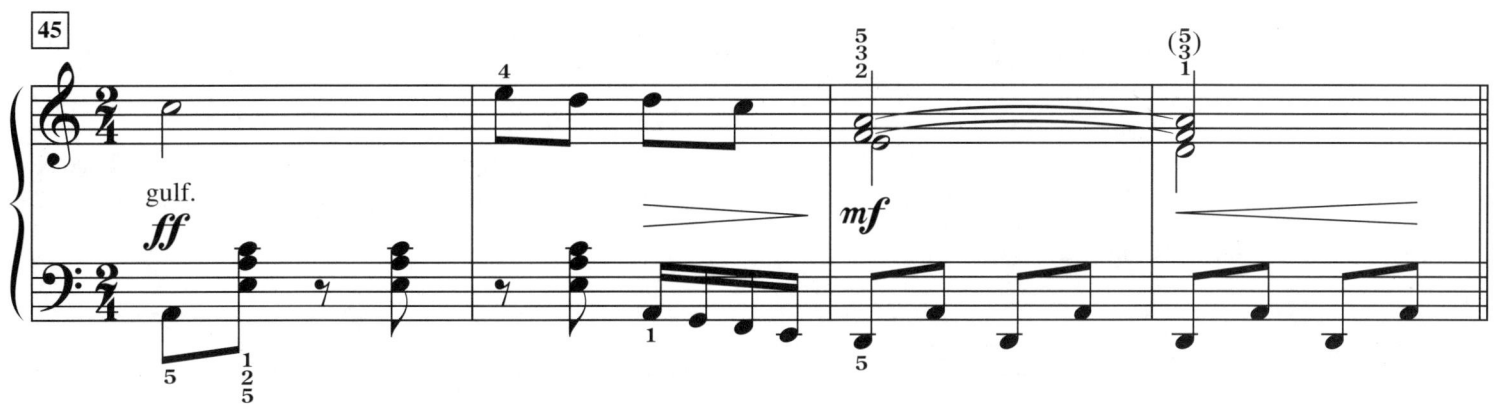

Double, dou - ble toil and trou - ble; fire_____ burn and caul - dron bub - ble.

Dou - ble, dou - ble toil and trou - ble; fi - re burn and caul - dron

bub - ble. Some - thing wick - ed this way comes!

EVERYTHING BURNS

Words and Music by Ben Moody
Arranged by Dan Coates

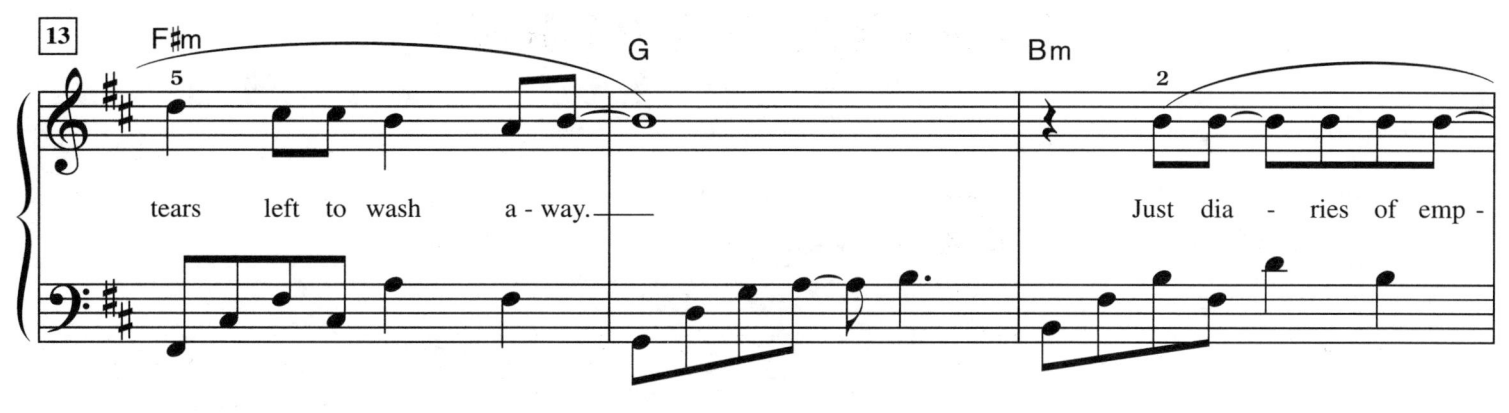

tears left to wash a-way. Just dia - ries of emp -

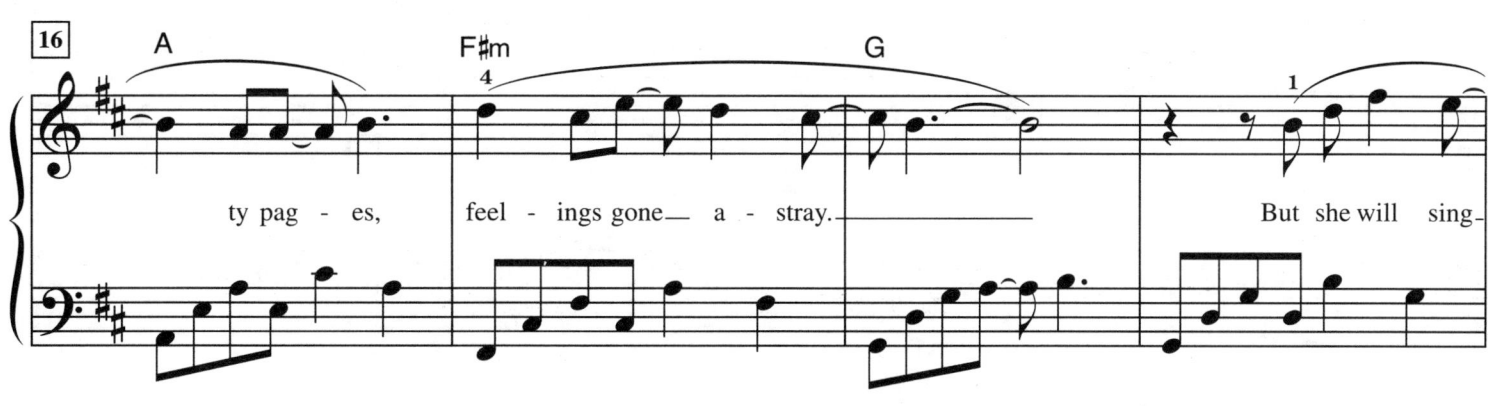

ty pag - es, feel - ings gone — a - stray. But she will sing —

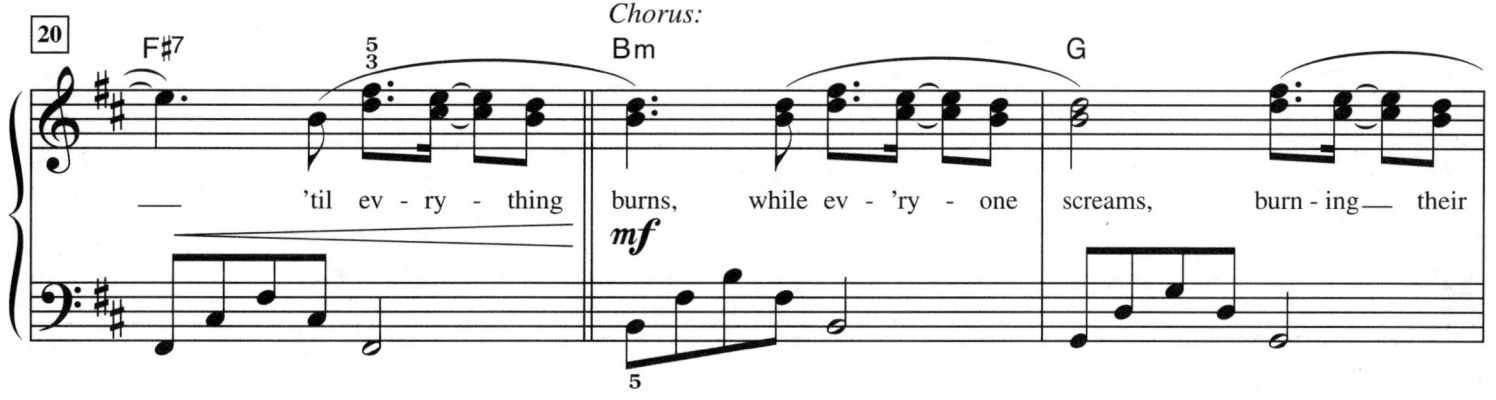

Chorus:

— 'til ev - ry - thing burns, while ev - 'ry - one screams, burn - ing — their

lies, burn - ing — my dreams. All of — this hate and all of — this

pain, I'll burn it____ all down as my an - ger rains,____ 'til ev - 'ry - thing

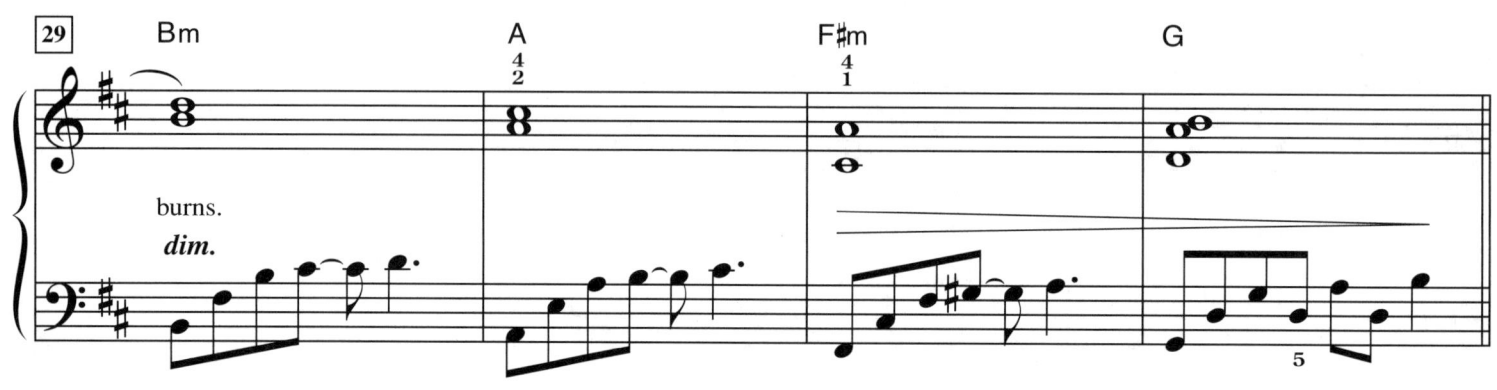

burns.
dim.

Verse:

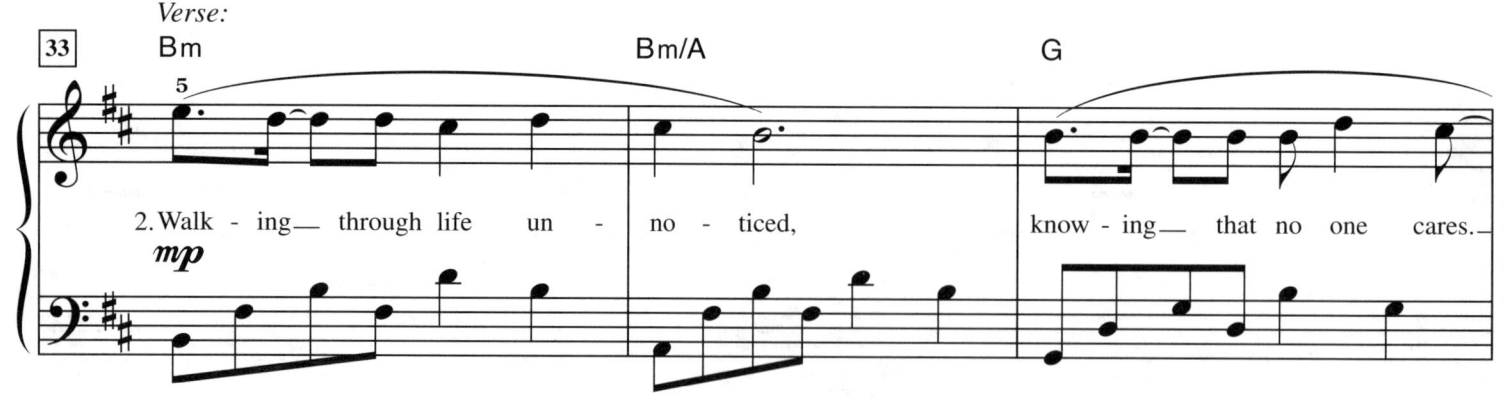

2. Walk - ing____ through life un - no - ticed, know - ing____ that no one cares.
mp

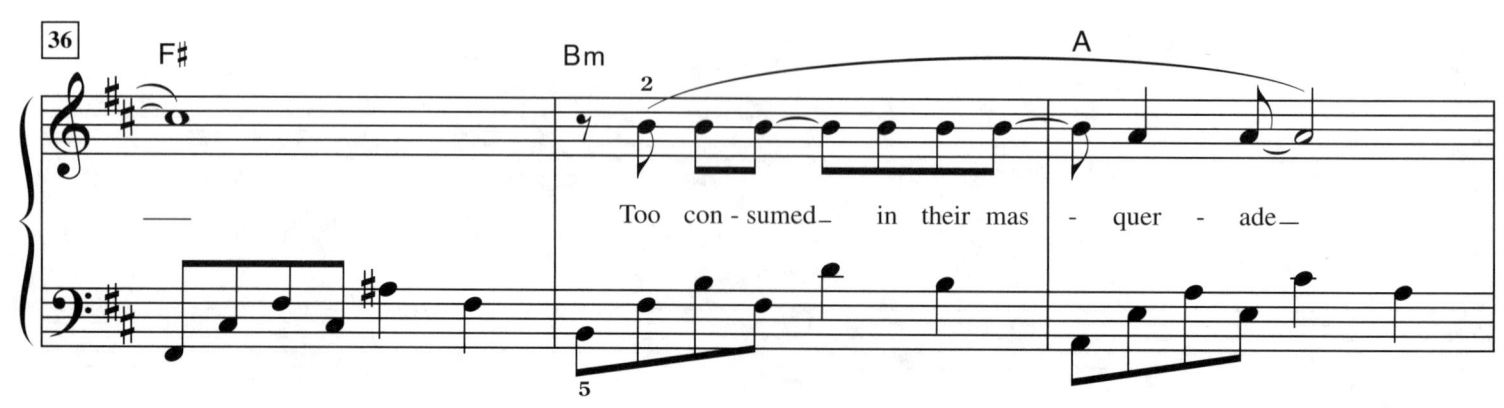

____ Too con - sumed____ in their mas - quer - ade____

no one sees— her there. And still— she sings

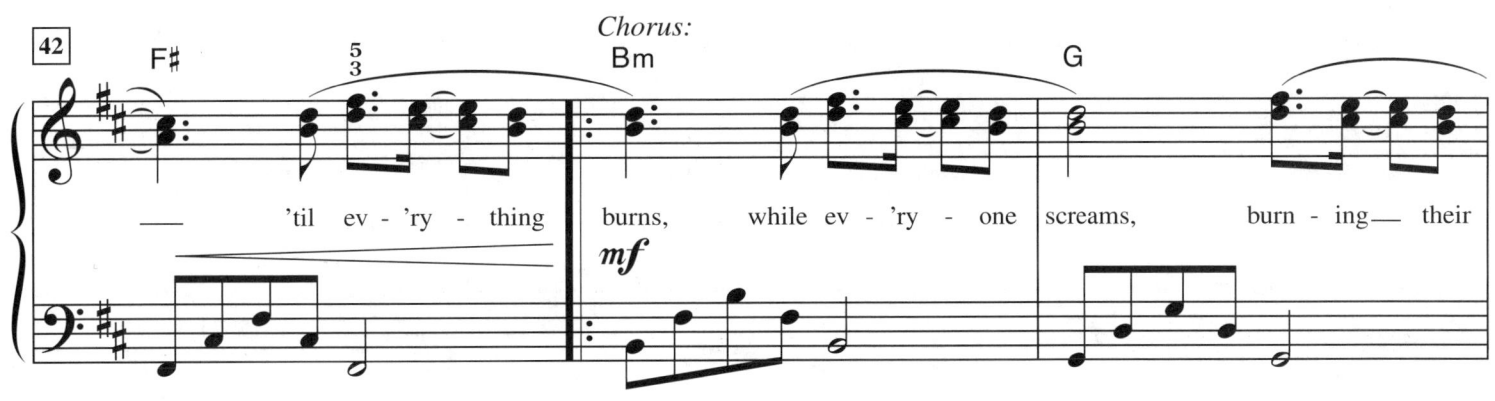

Chorus:

— 'til ev-'ry - thing burns, while ev-'ry - one screams, burn-ing— their

lies, burn-ing— my dreams. All of— this hate and all of— this

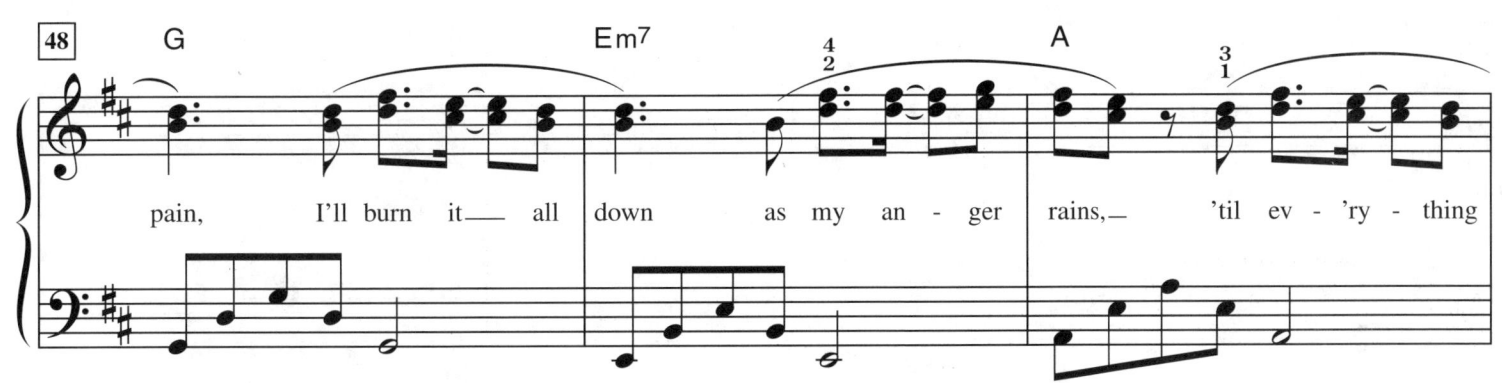

pain, I'll burn it— all down as my an - ger rains,— 'til ev-'ry - thing

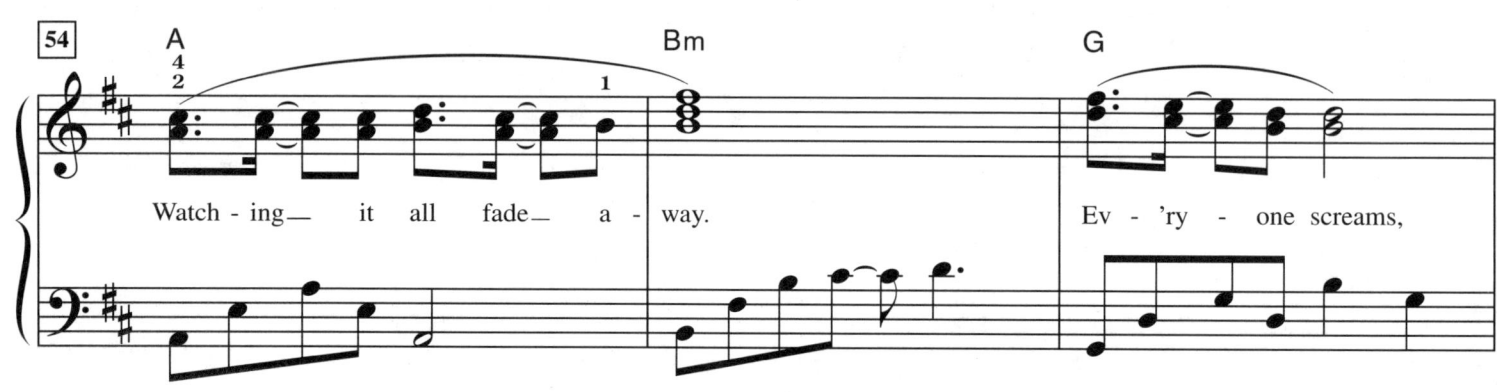

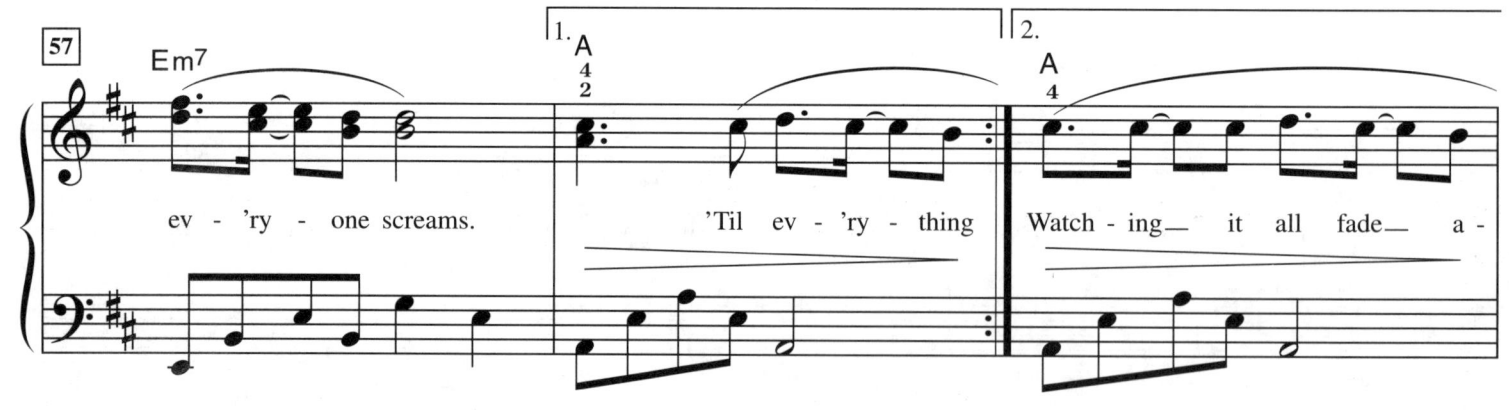

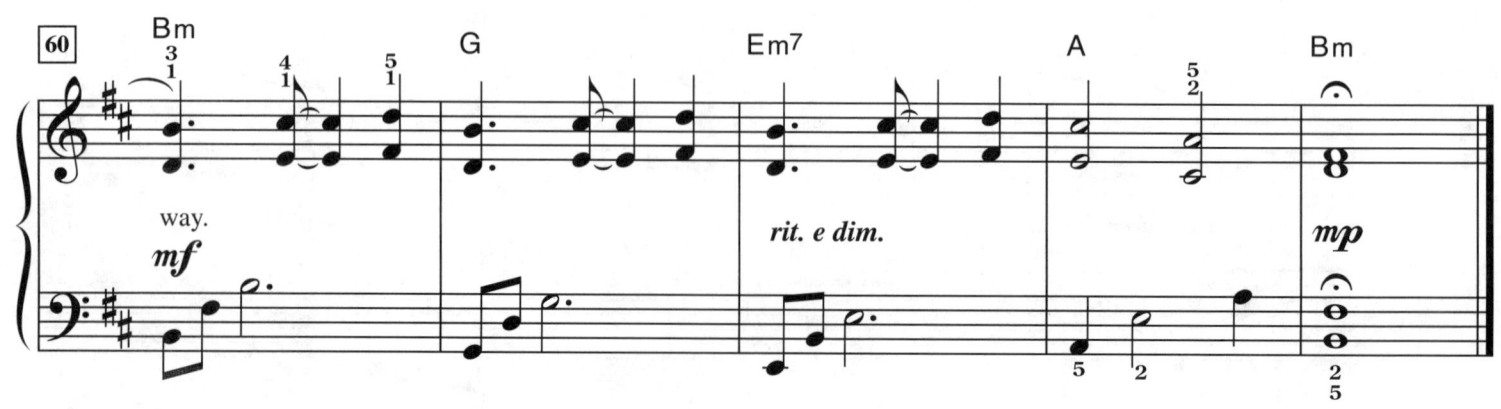

FOR YOU I WILL

Words and Music by Diane Warren
Arranged by Dan Coates

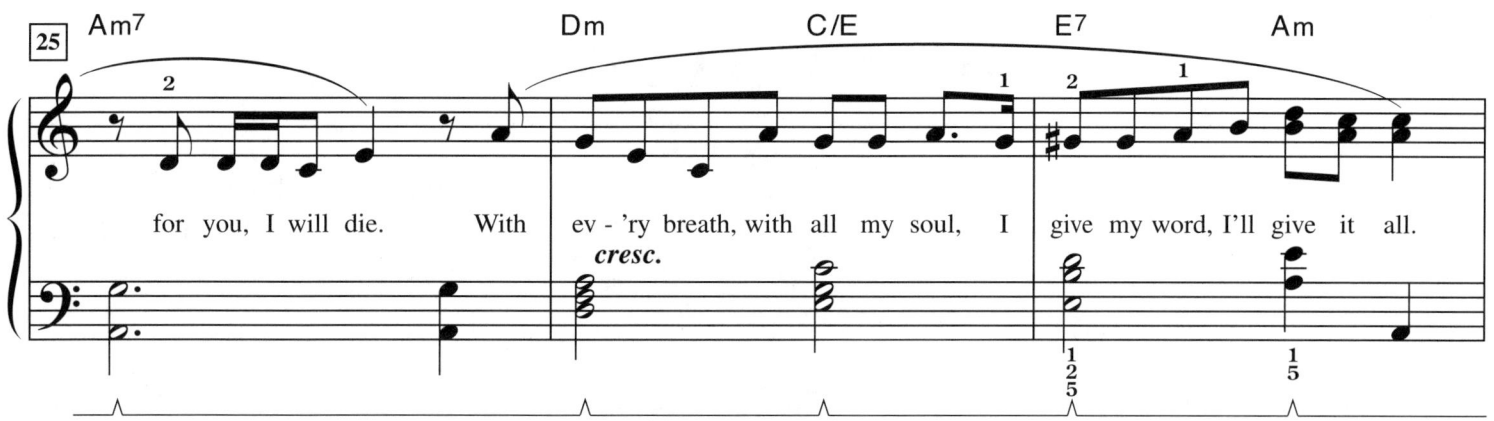

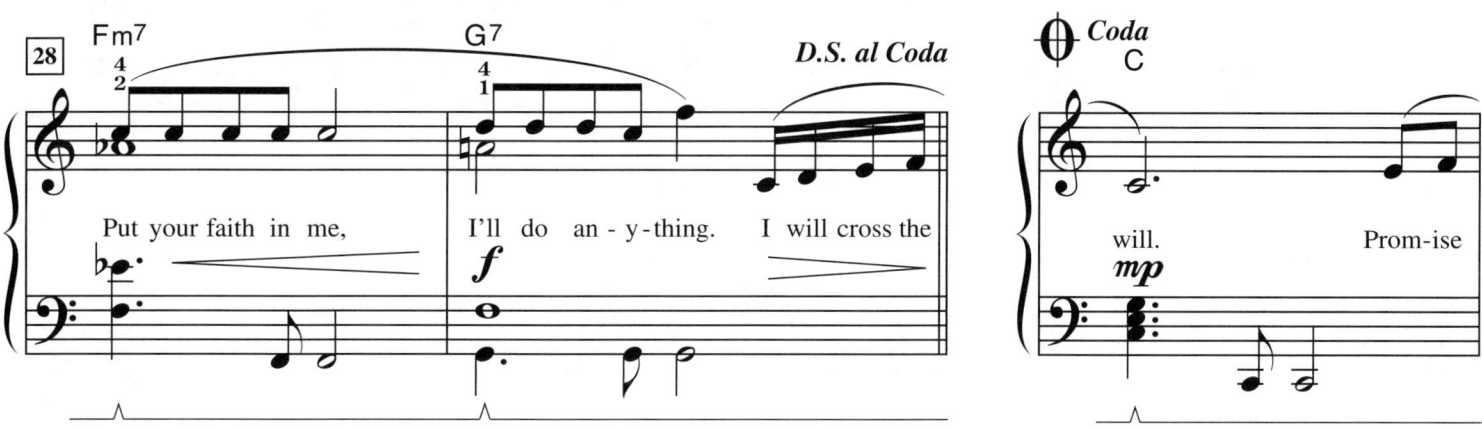

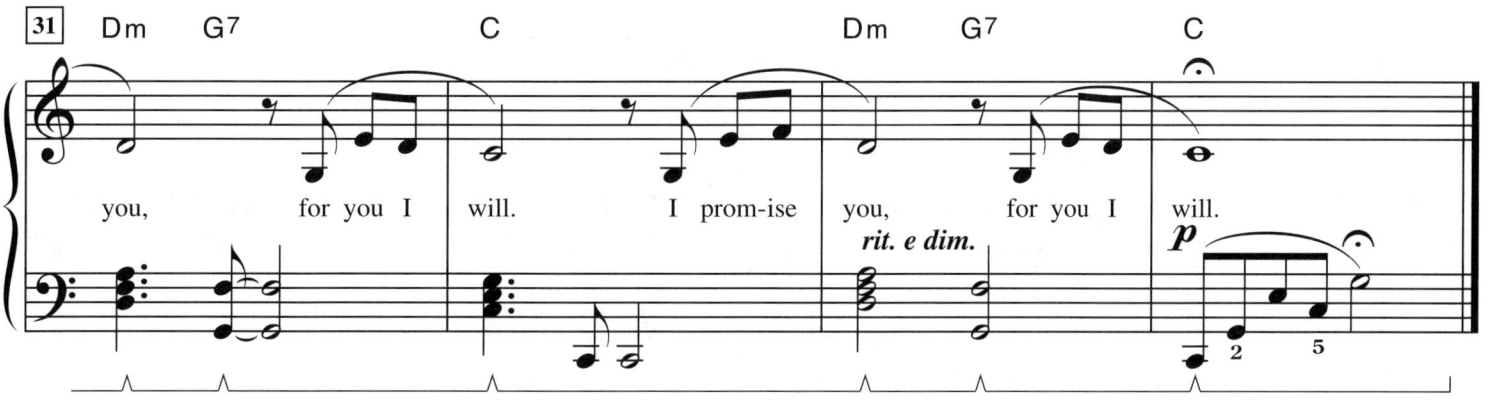

Verse 2:
I will shield your heart from the rain,
I won't let no harm come your way.
Oh, these arms will be your shelter,
No, these arms won't let you down.
If there is a mountain to move,
I will move that mountain for you.
I'm here for you, I'm here forever.
I will be a fortress, tall and strong.
I'll keep you safe, I'll stand beside you,
Right or wrong.
(To Chorus:)

HOW DO I LIVE

Words and Music by Diane Warren
Arranged by Dan Coates

Verse 2:
Without you, there'd be no sun in my sky,
There would be no love in my life,
There'd be no world left for me.
And I, baby, I don't know what I would do,
I'd be lost if I lost you.
If you ever leave,
Baby, you would take away everything
Real in my life.
And tell me now...
(To Chorus):

MUSIC OF MY HEART

Words and Music by Diane Warren
Arranged by Dan Coates

HOGWARTS' HYMN

By Patrick Doyle
Arranged by Dan Coates

Slowly, with expression (♩ = 69)

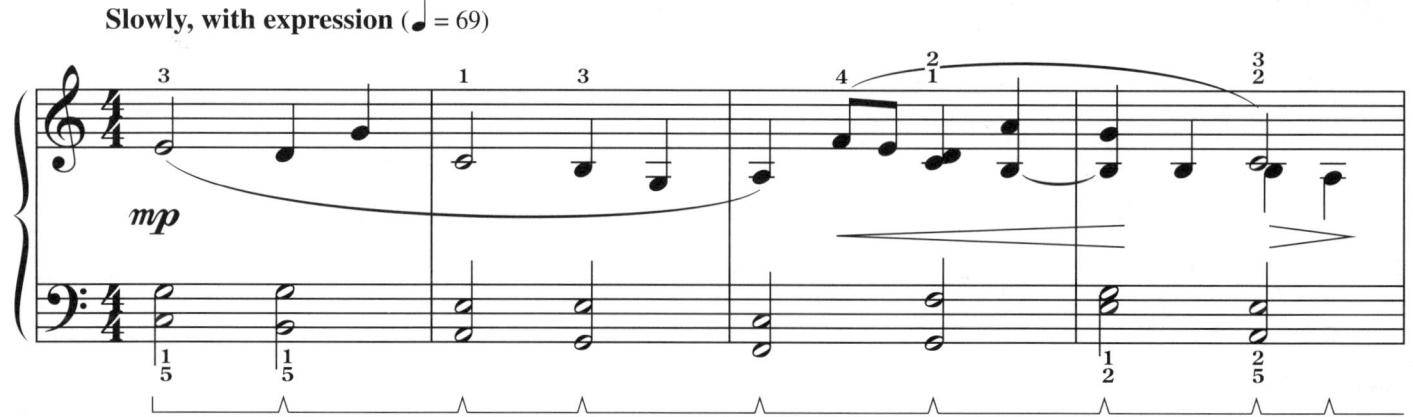

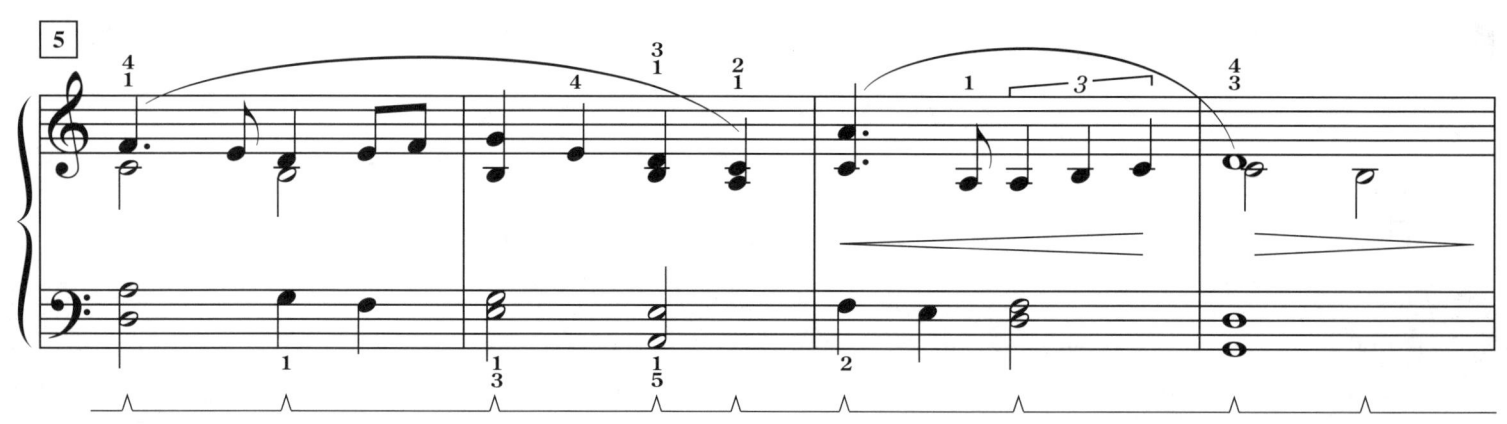

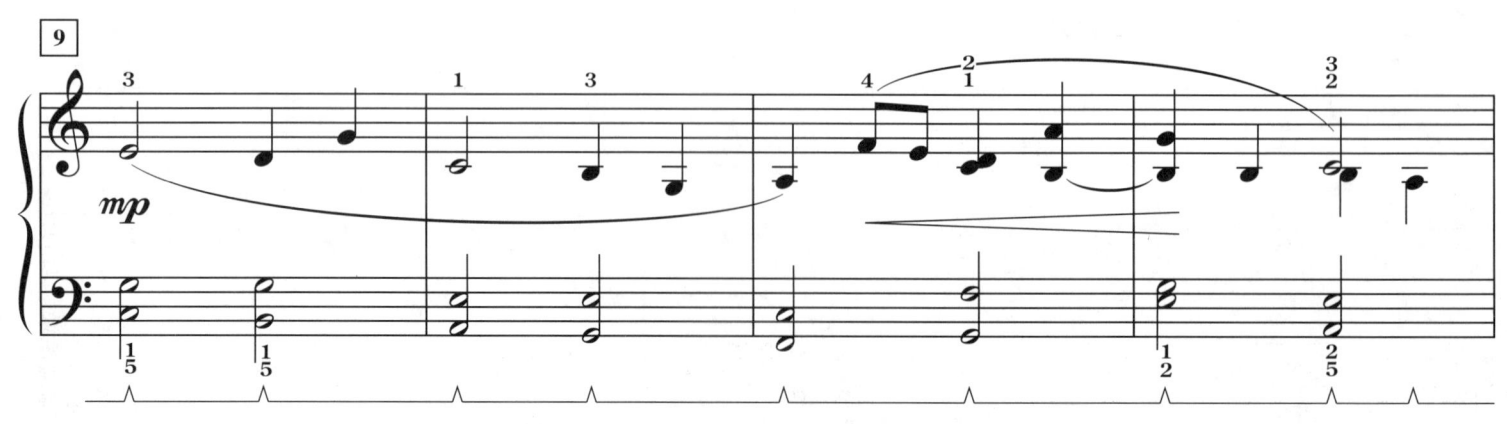

I BELIEVE IN YOU AND ME

Words and Music by Sandy Linzer
and David Wolfert
Arranged by Dan Coates

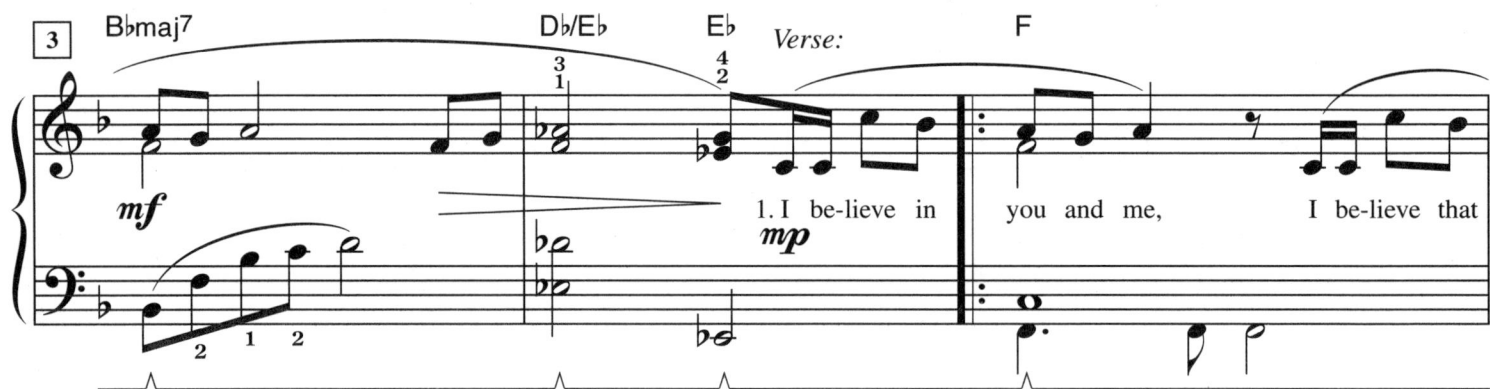

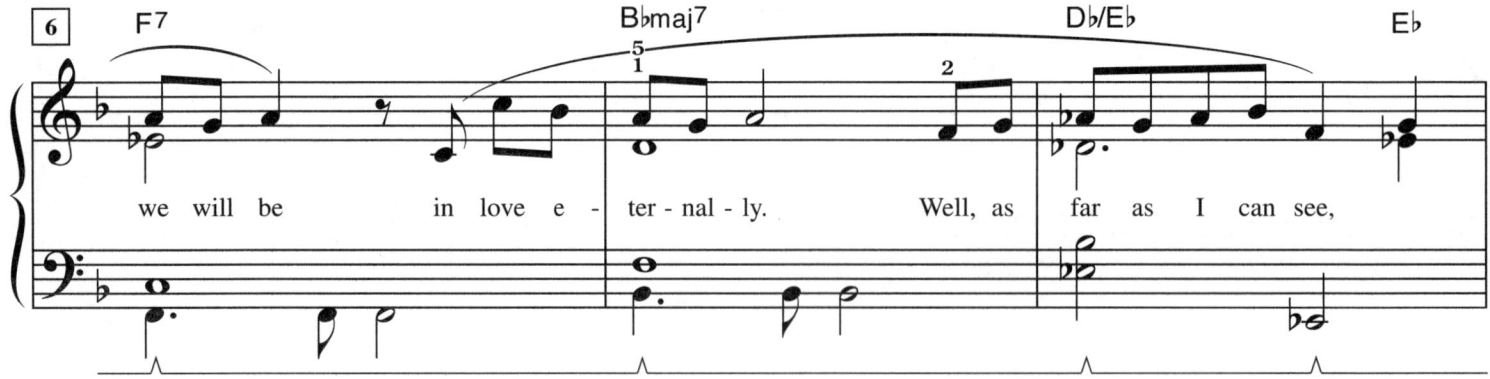

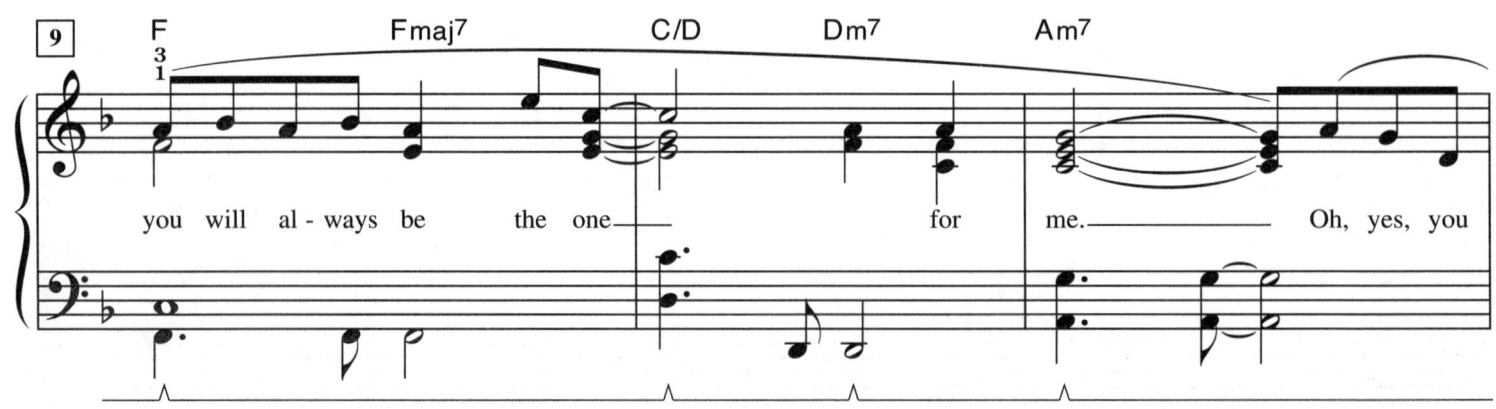

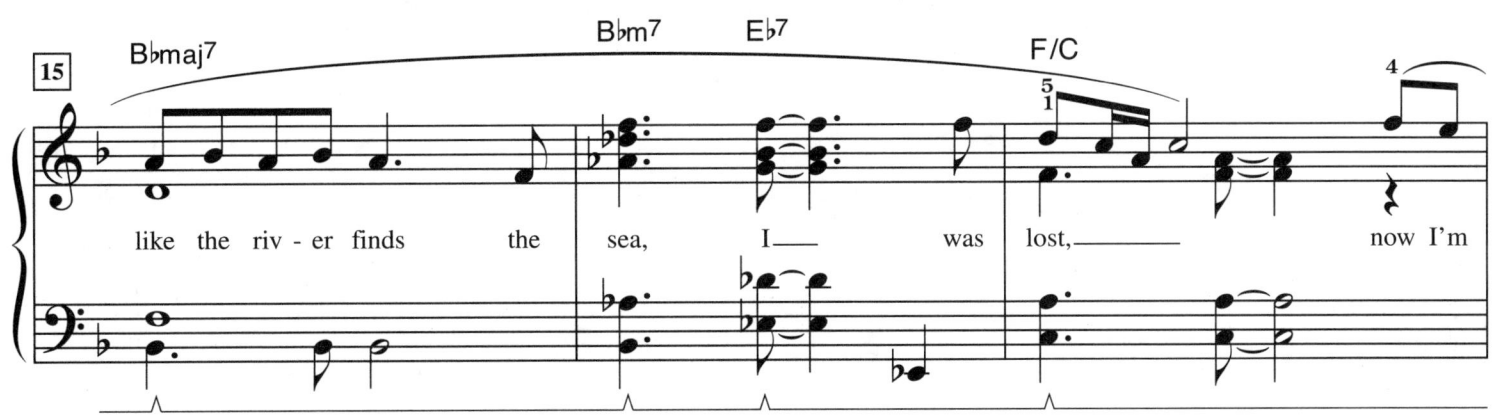

I would play the fool for - ev - er just to be with you for - ev - er.

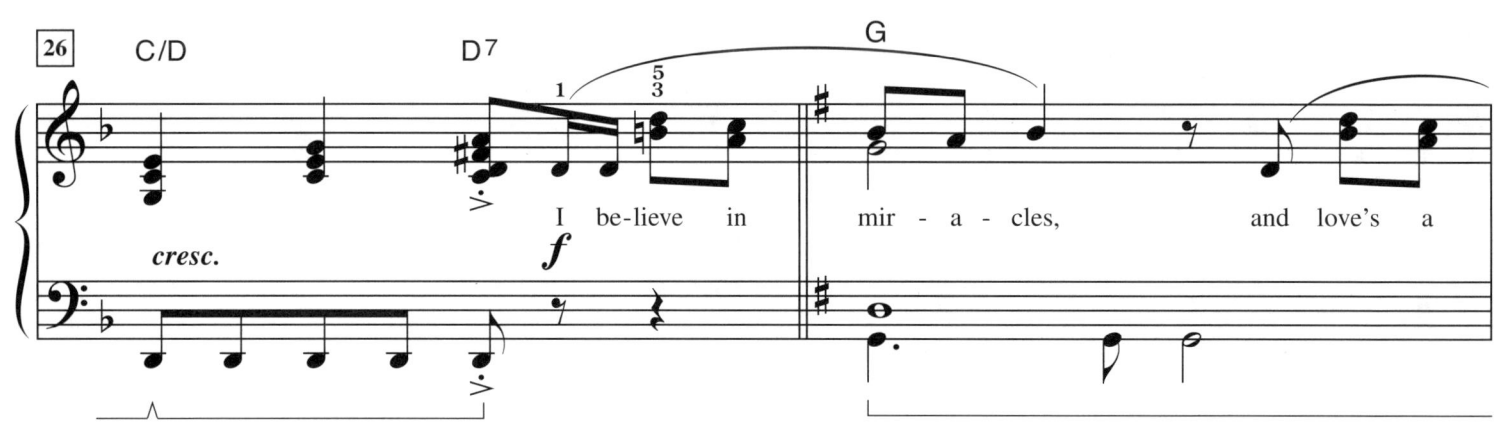

I be - lieve in mir - a - cles, and love's a

mir - a - cle. And yes, ba - by, you're my dream— come true. I was

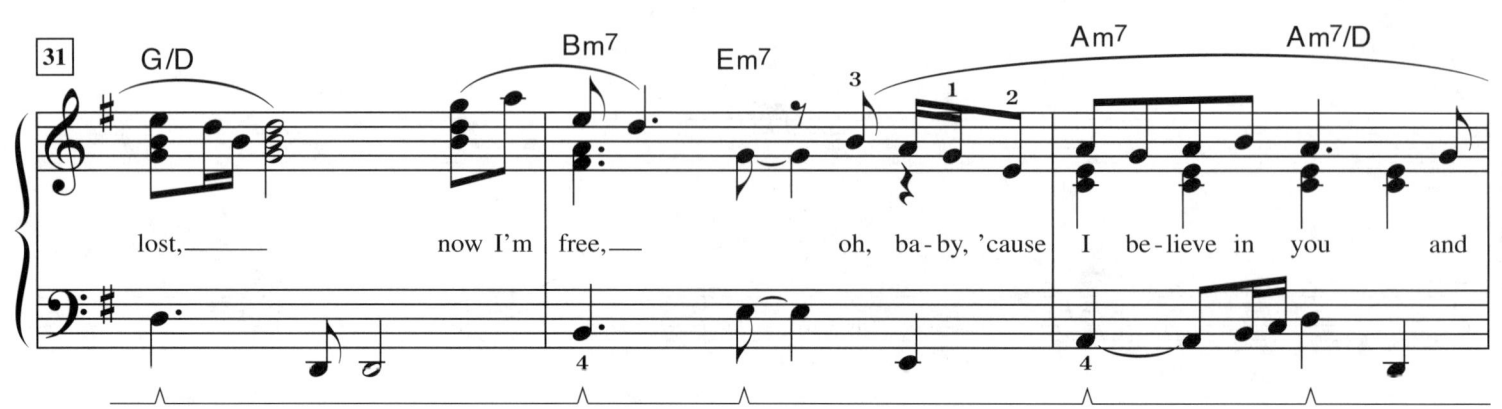

lost,— now I'm free,— oh, ba - by, 'cause I be - lieve in you and

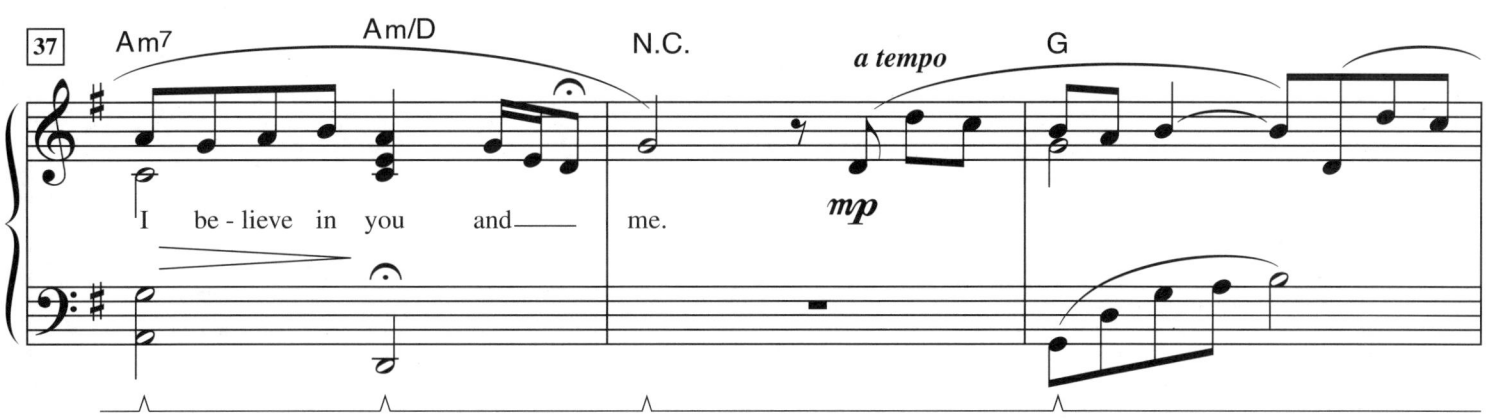

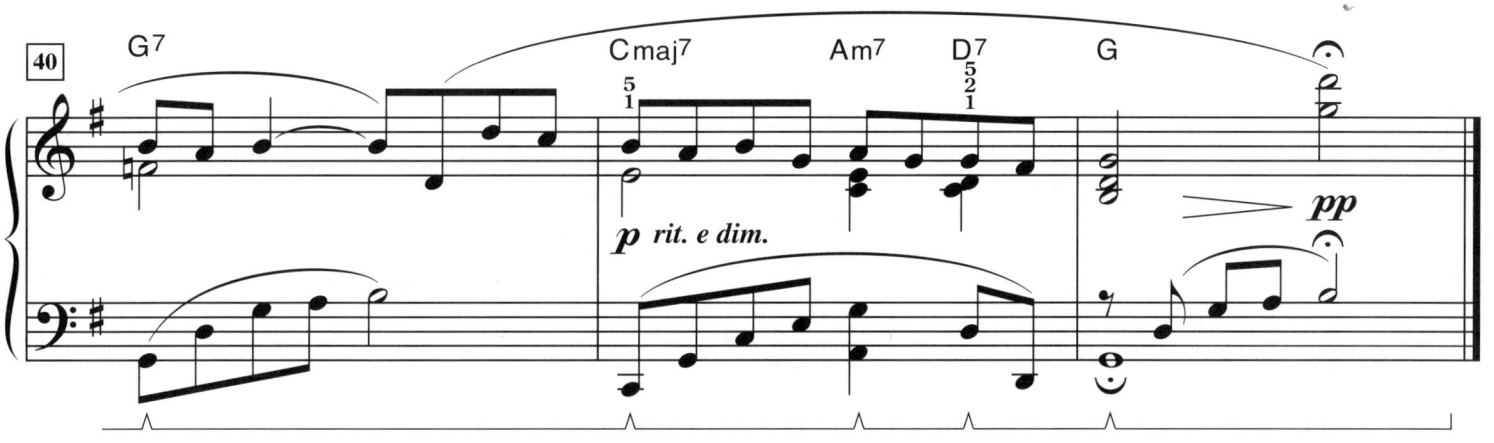

Verse 2:
I will never leave your side,
I will never hurt your pride.
When all the chips are down,
I will always be around
Just to be right where you are, my love.
Oh, I love you, boy.
I will never leave you out,
I will always let you in
To places no one has ever been.
Deep inside, can't you see?
I believe in you and me.

INTO THE WEST

Words and Music by Fran Walsh,
Howard Shore, Annie Lennox
Arranged by Dan Coates

now. Dream of the ones who came be - fore.

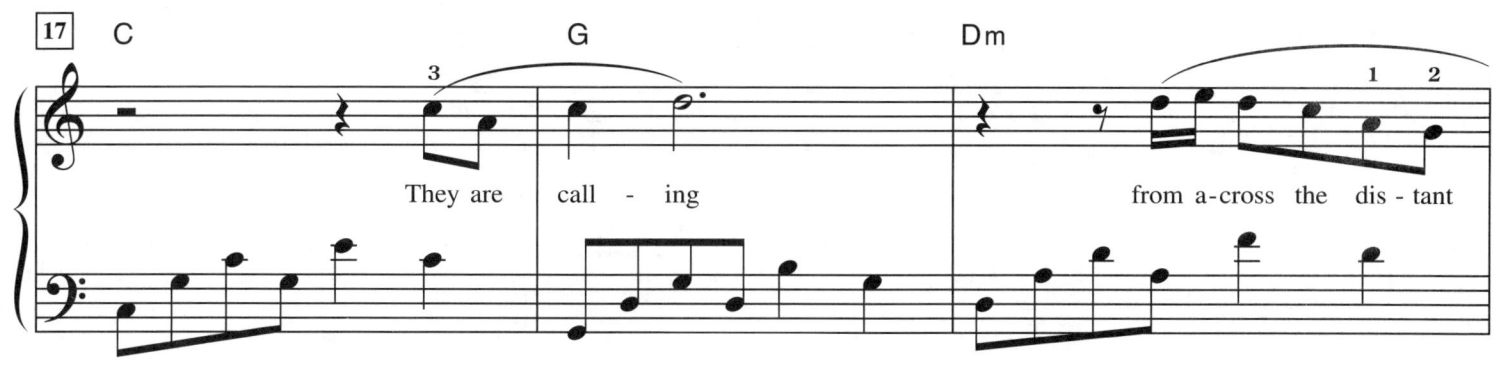

They are call - ing from a-cross the dis - tant

shore. *mp* Why do you weep?

What are these tears up - on your face? Soon you will see

ped. simile

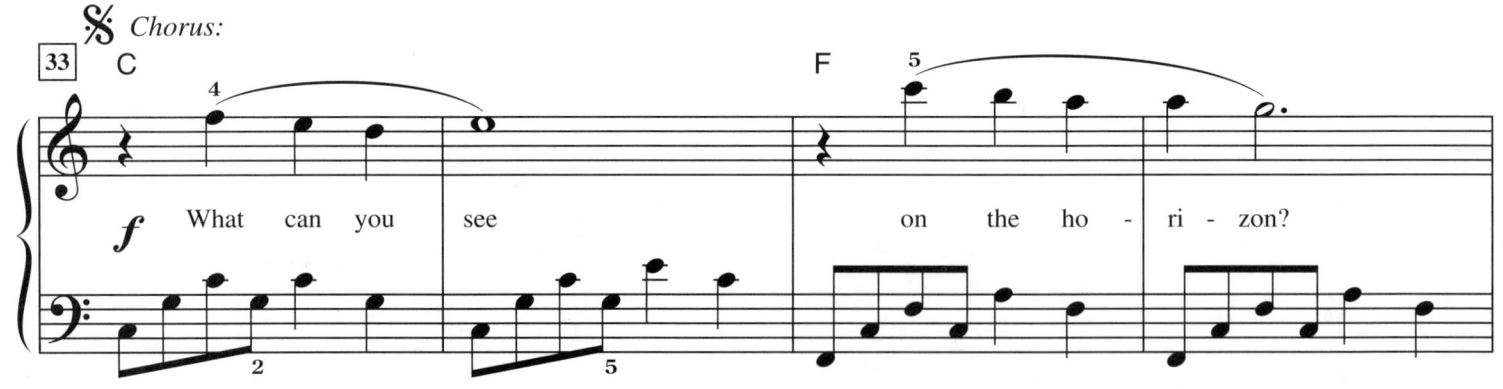

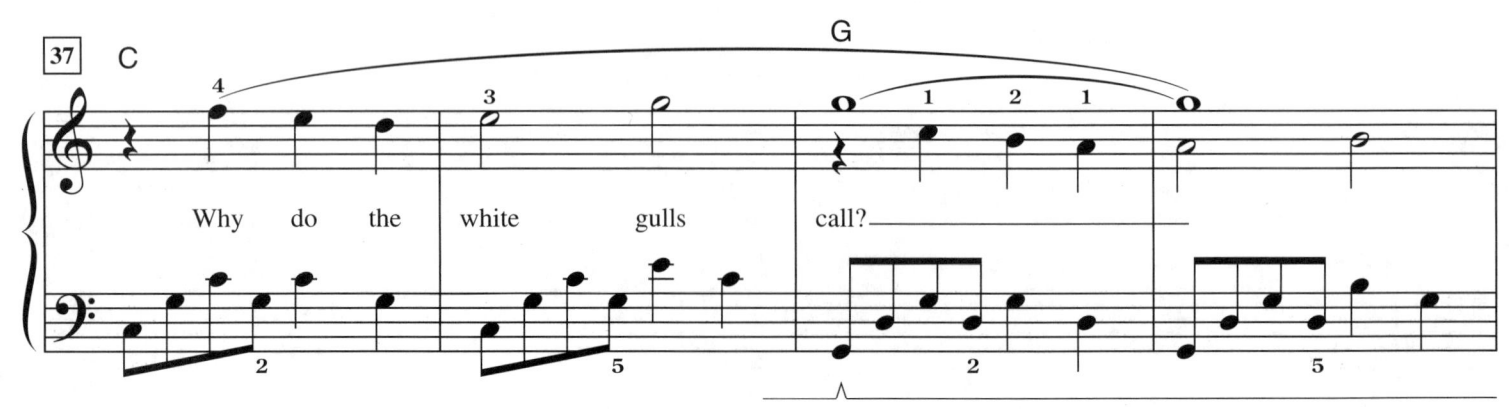

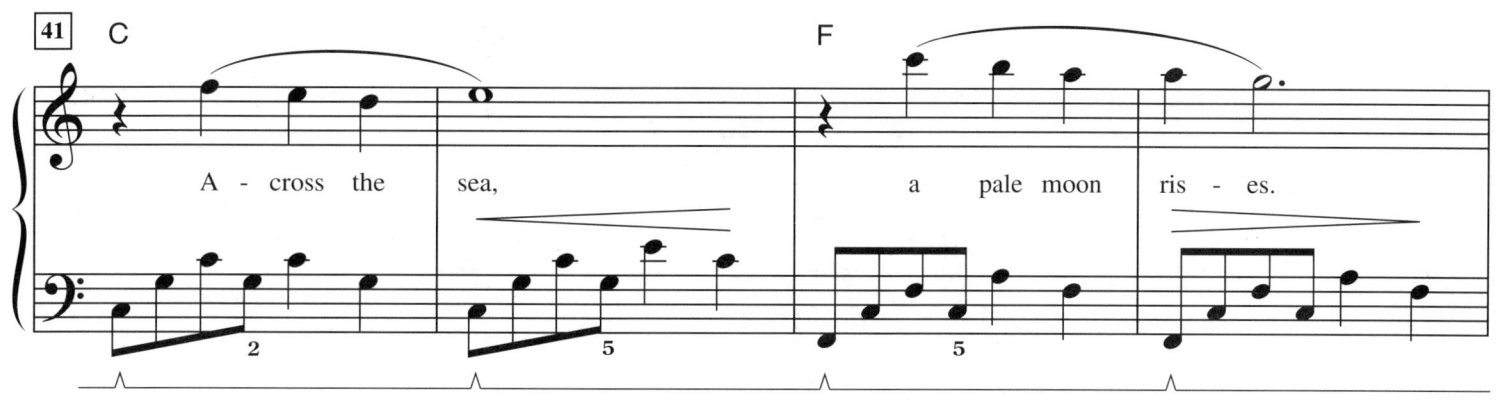

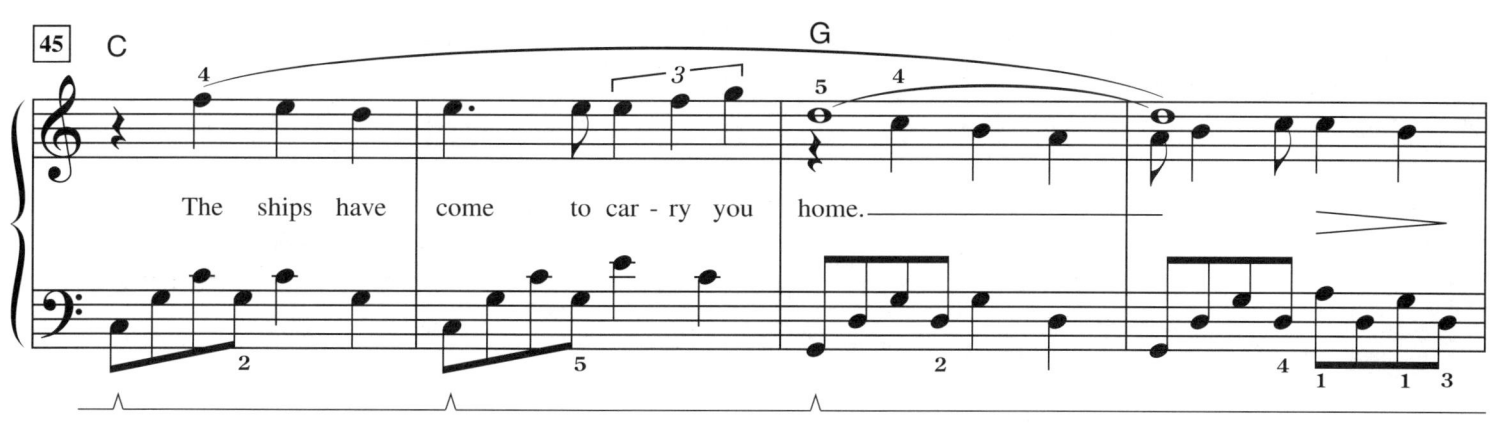

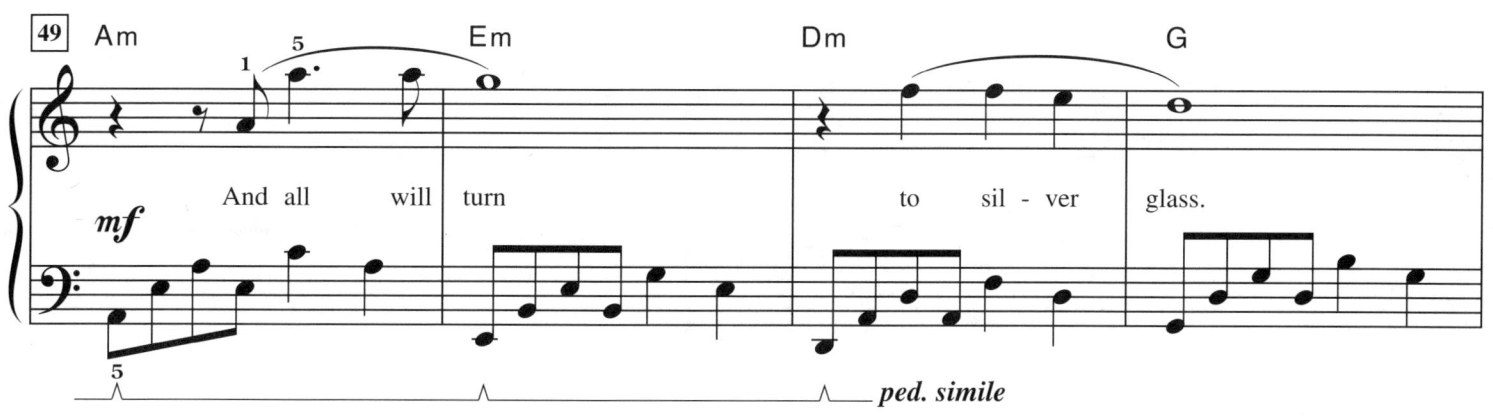

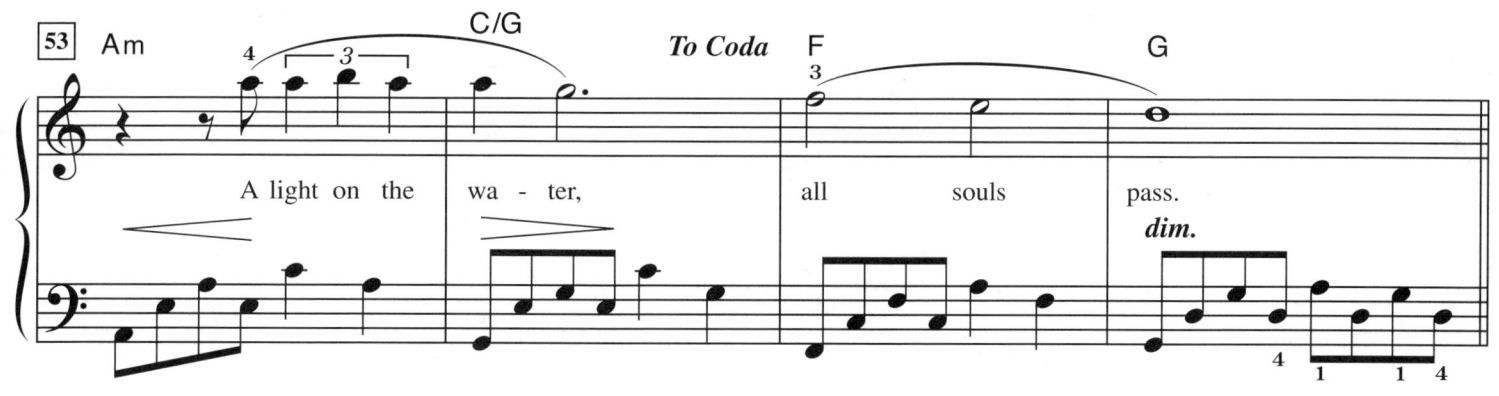

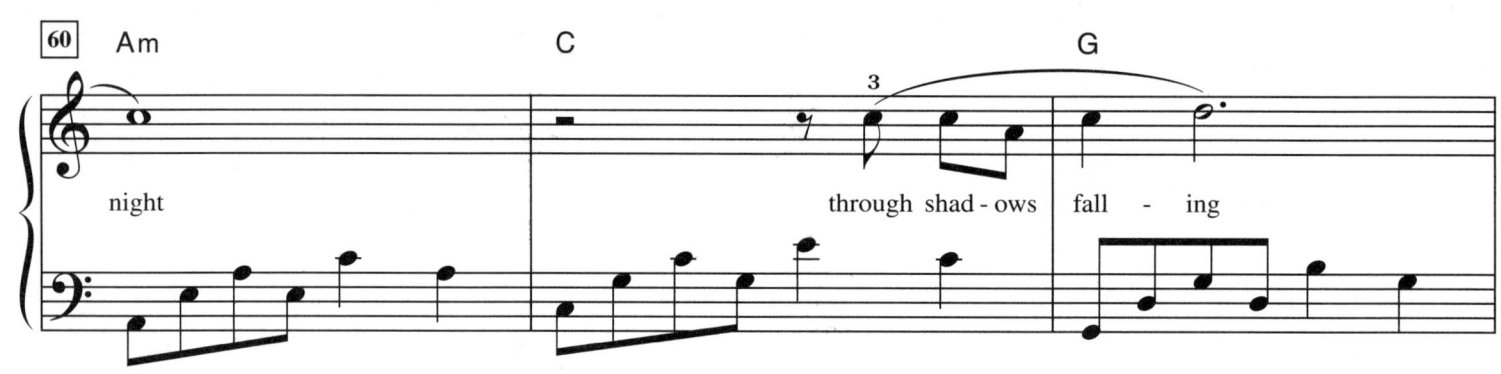

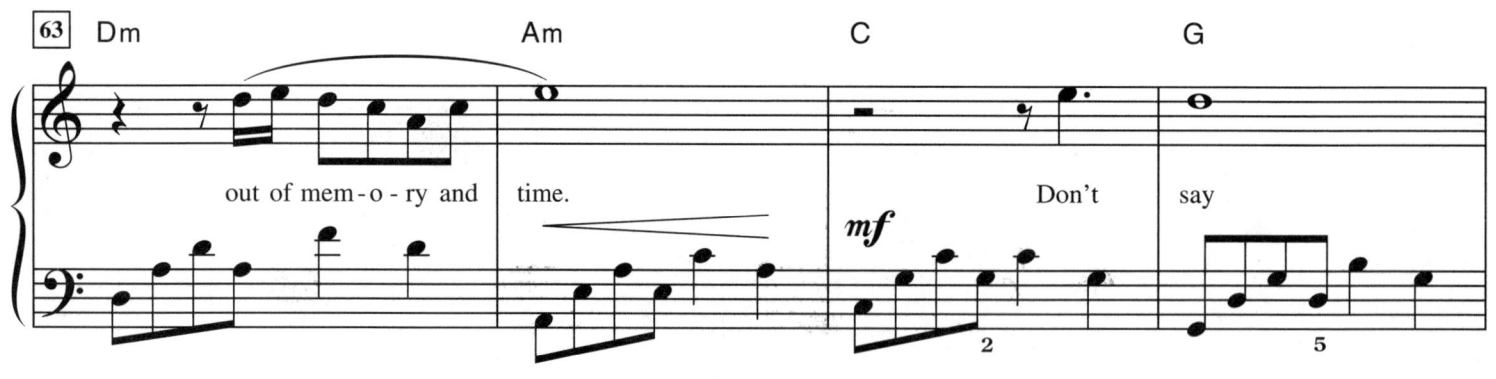

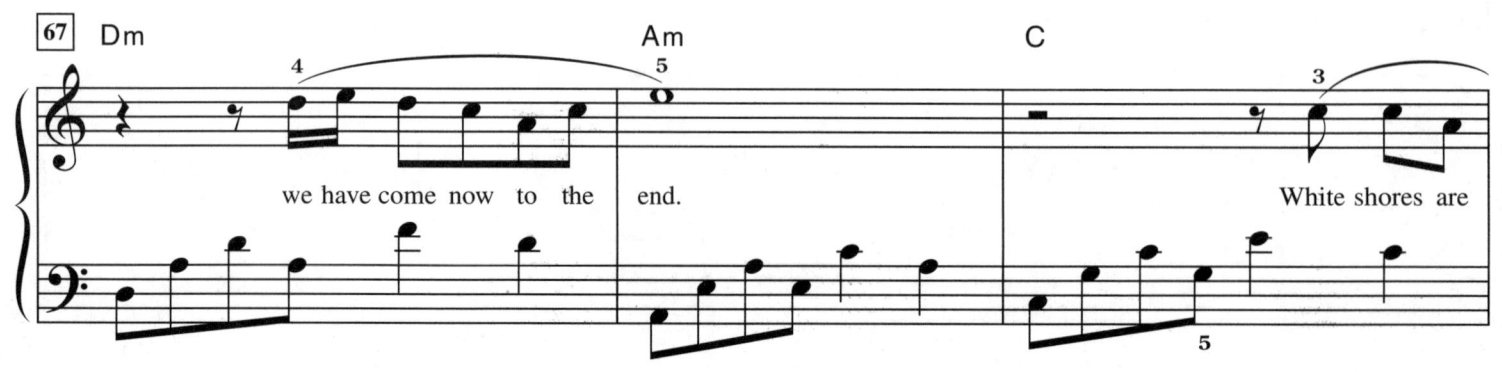

call - ing. You and I will meet a - gain. And you'll be

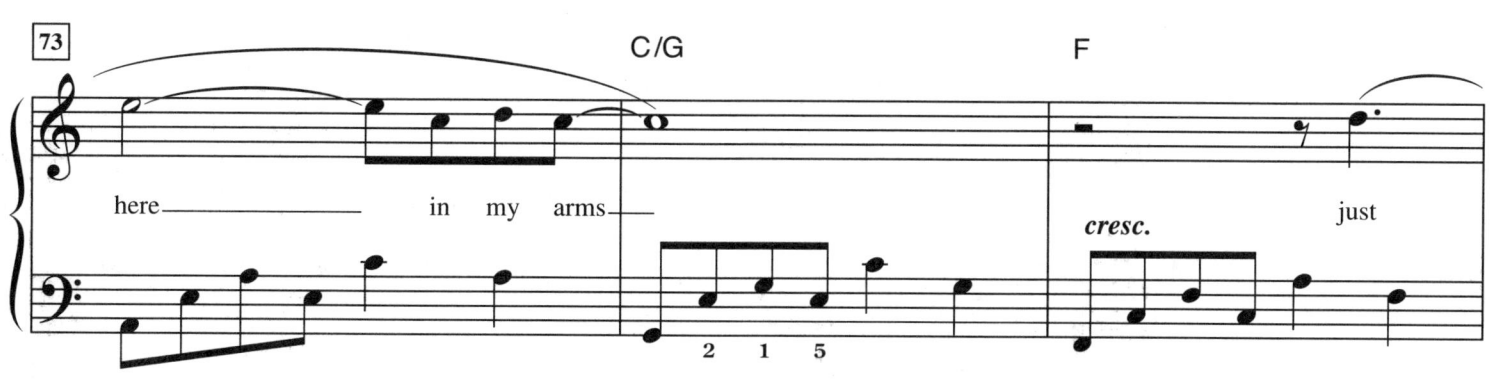

here _____ in my arms ___ *cresc.* just

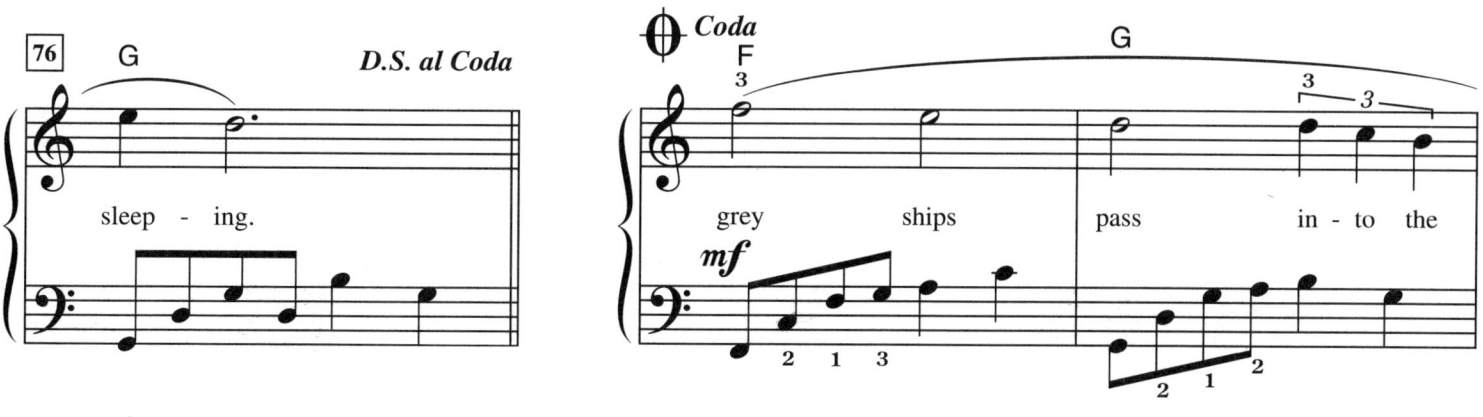

sleep - ing. *D.S. al Coda* *Coda* grey ships pass in - to the *mf*

West. *mp rit. e dim.* *p*

MAGIC WORKS

By Jarvis Cocker
Arranged by Dan Coates

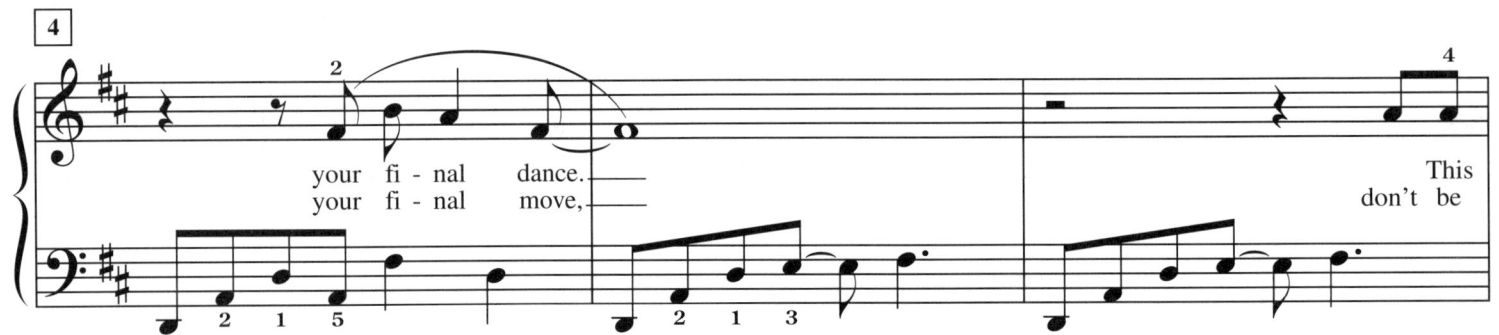

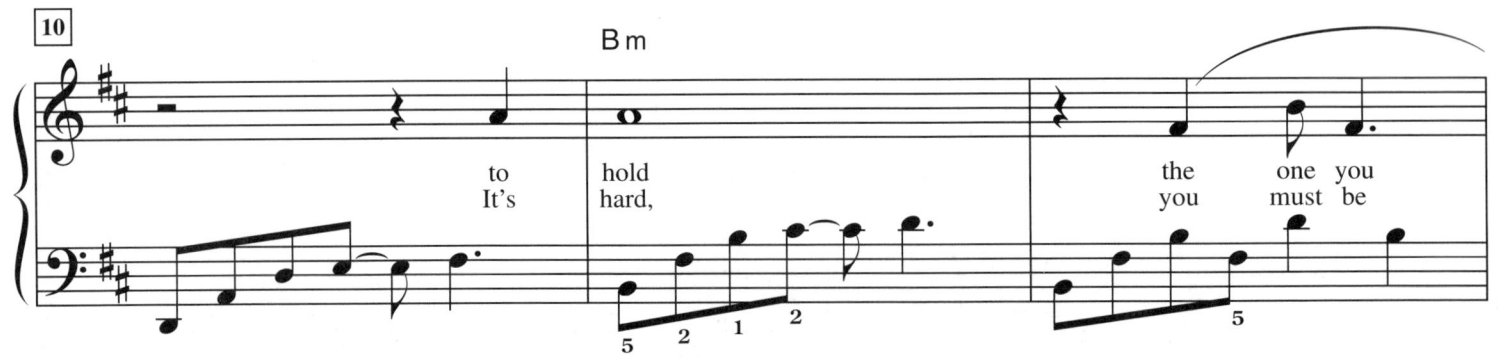

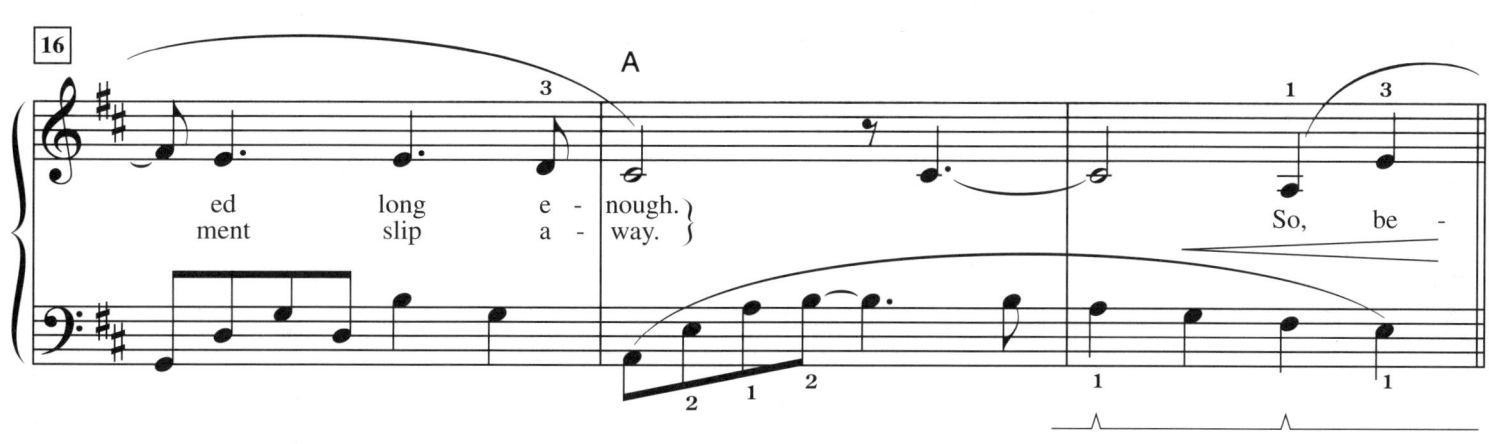

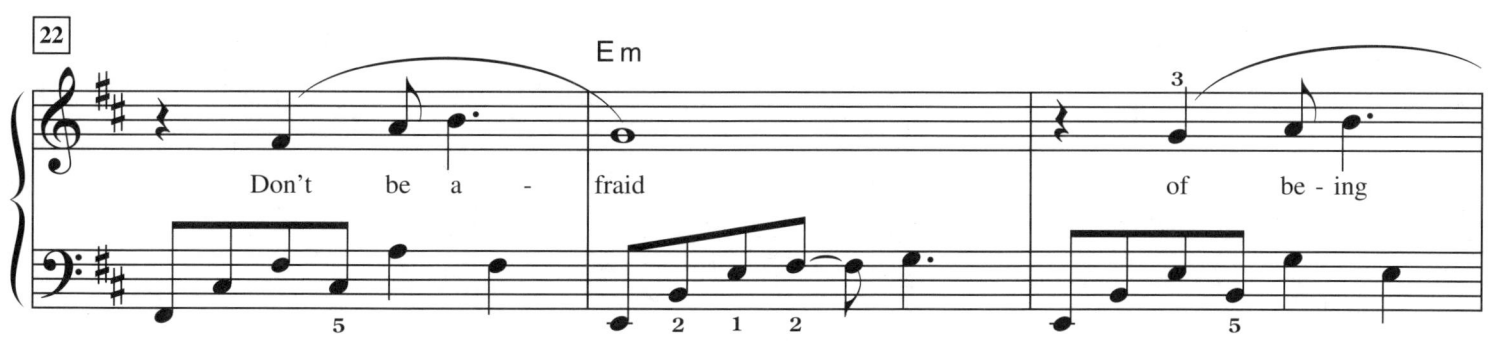

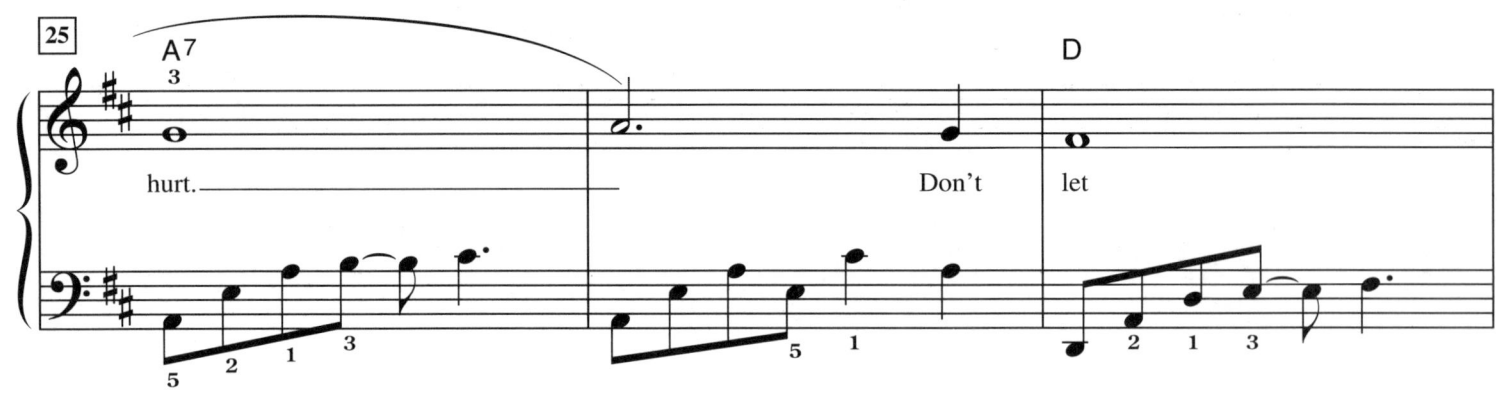

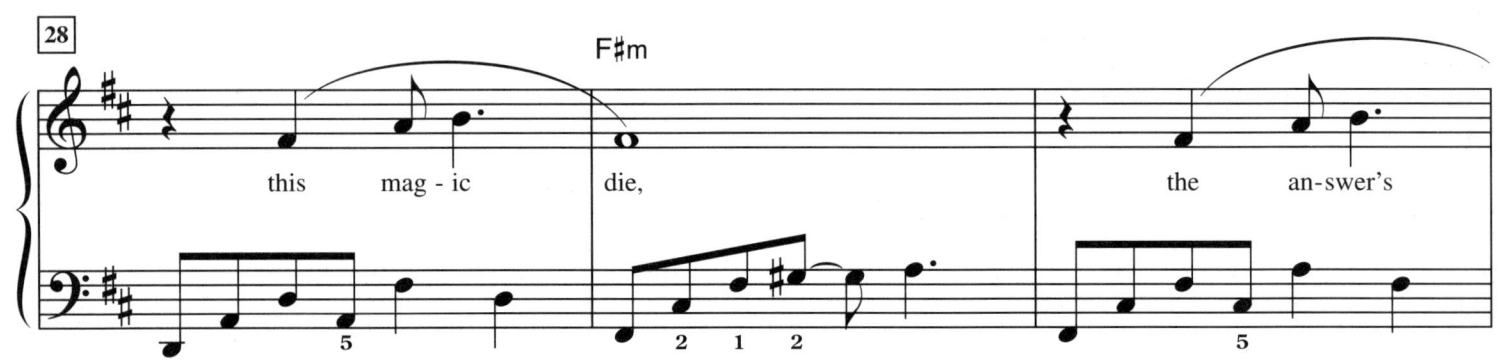

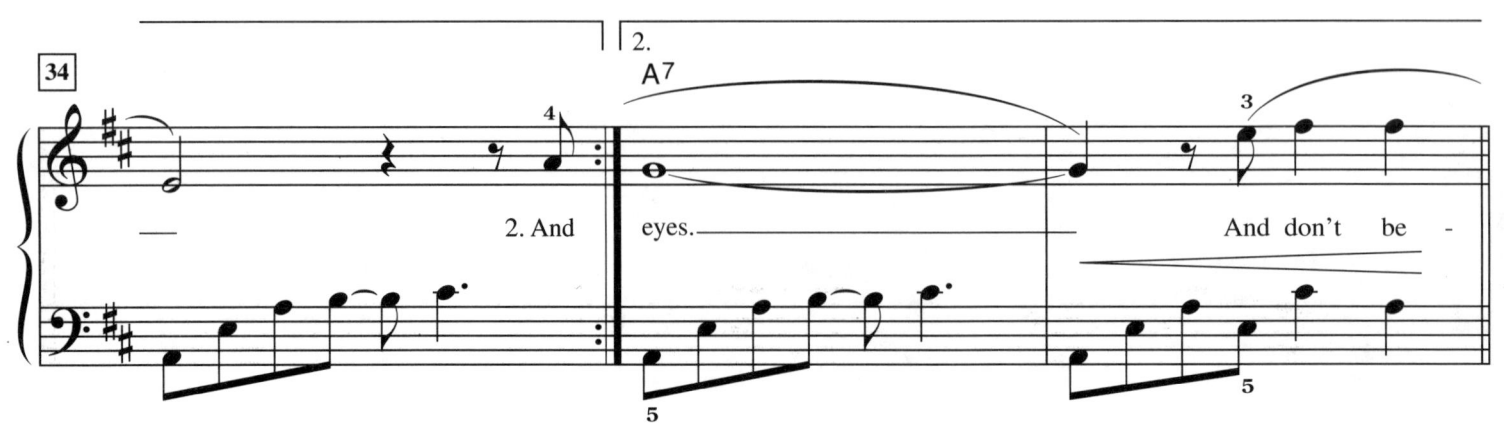

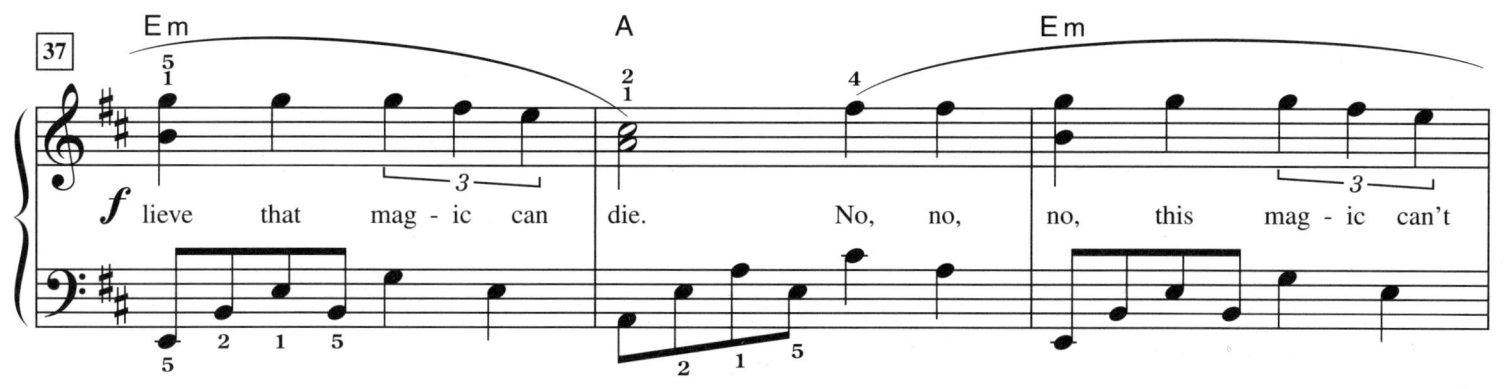

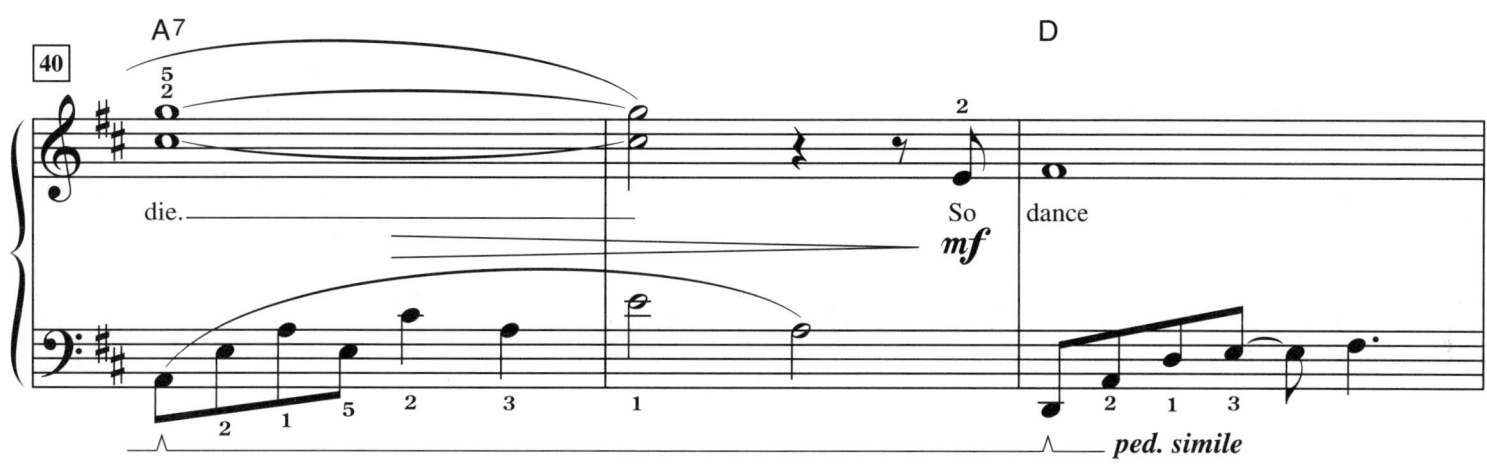

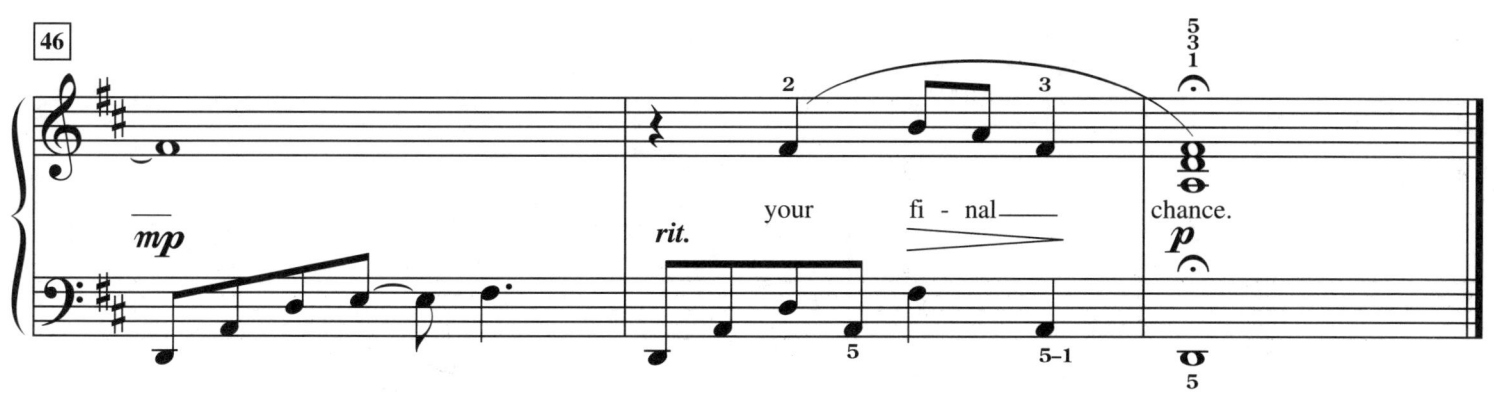

STAYIN' ALIVE

Words and Music by Barry Gibb,
Maurice Gibb and Robin Gibb
Arranged by Dan Coates

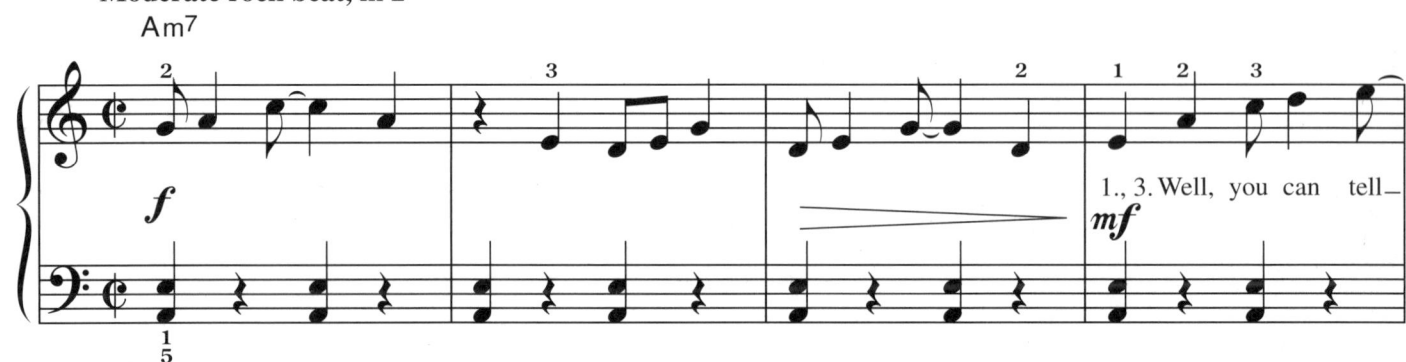

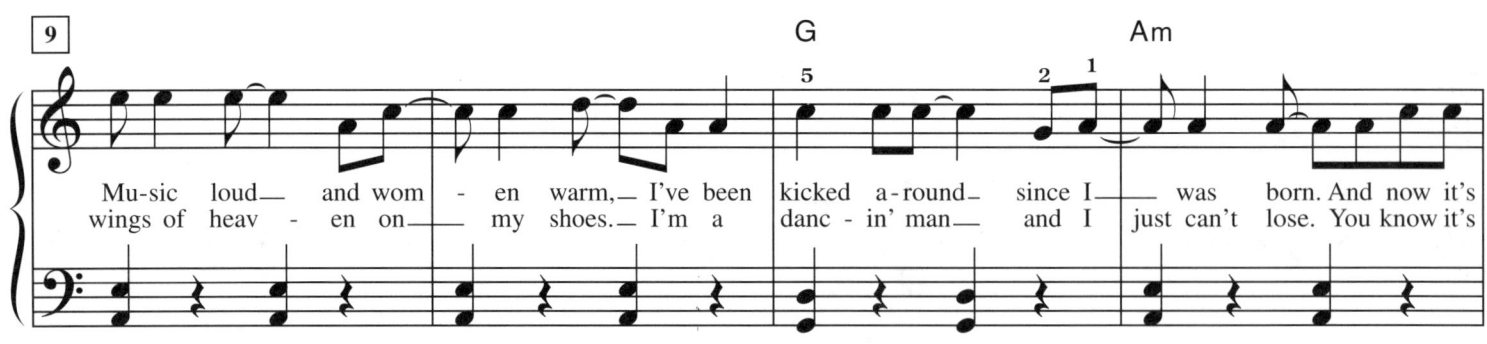

TAKE MY BREATH AWAY

By Giorgio Moroder and Tom Whitlock
Arranged by Dan Coates

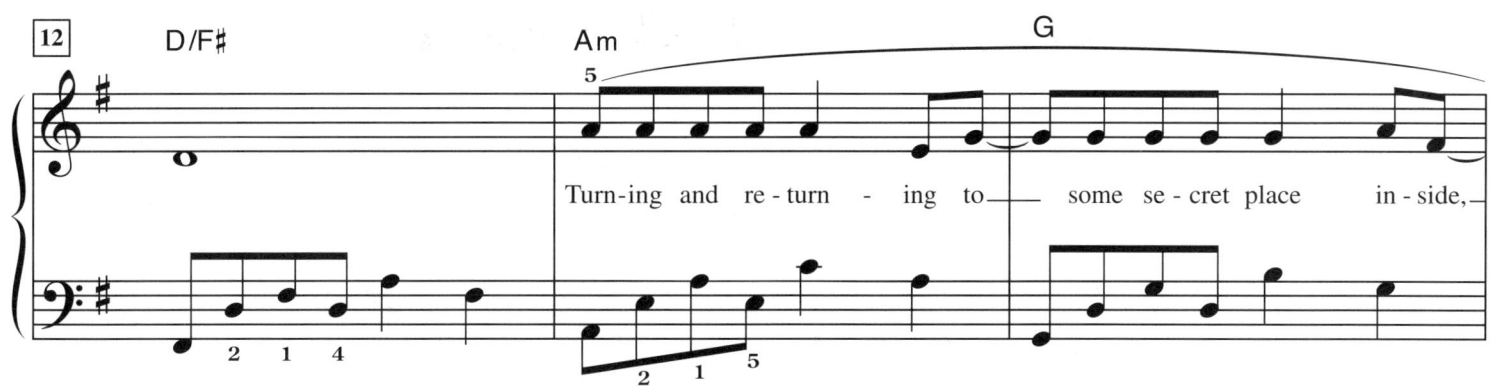

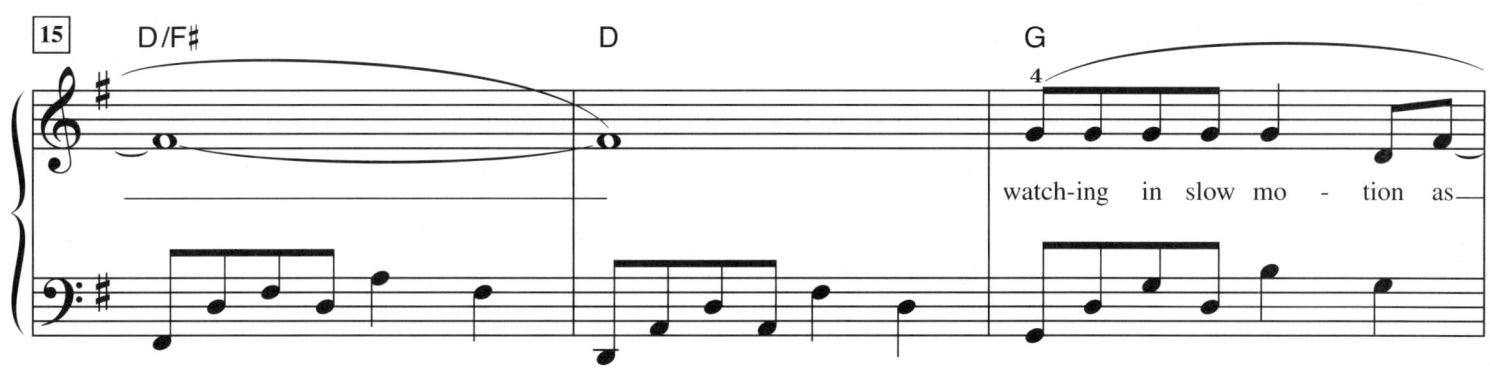

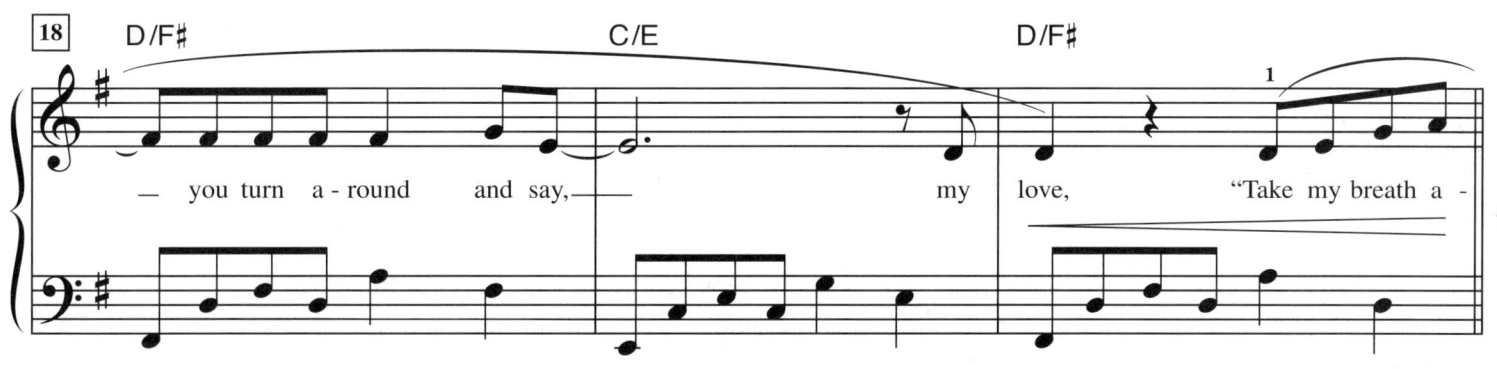

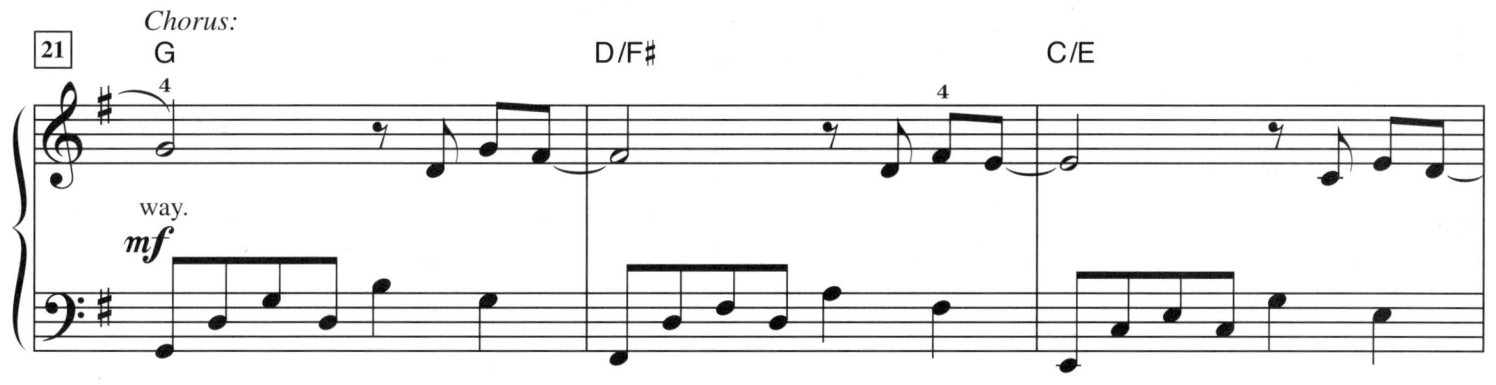

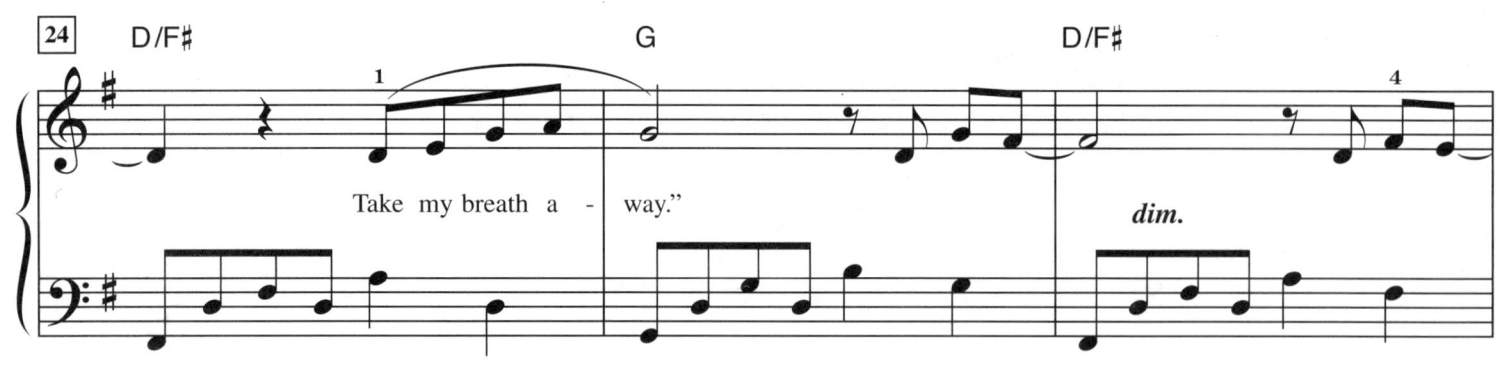

Take my breath a - way."

dim.

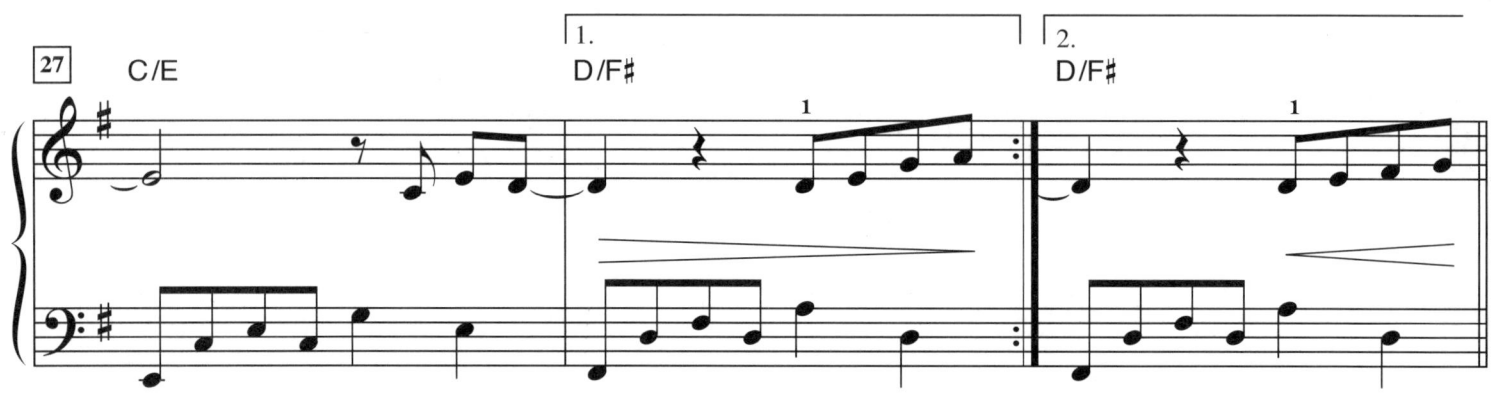

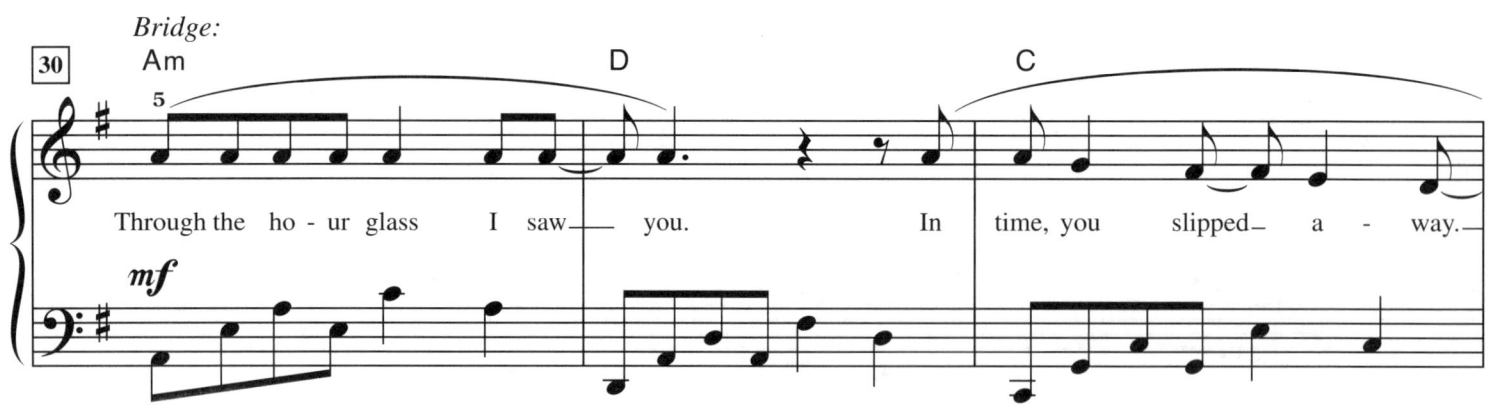

Bridge:

Through the ho - ur glass I saw — you. In time, you slipped — a - way. —

mf

— When the mir - ror crashed, I called — you and

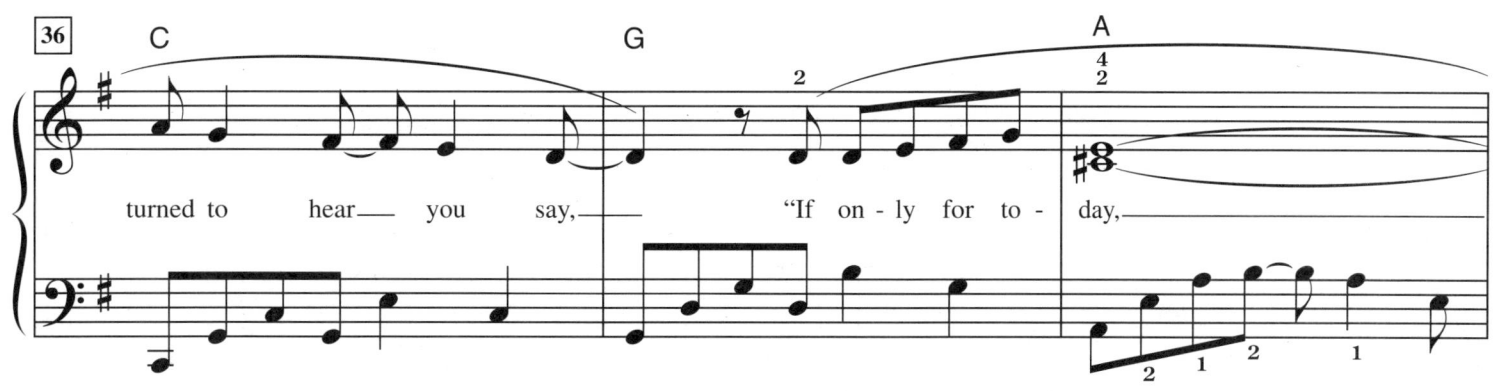

turned to hear— you say,— "If on - ly for to - day,—

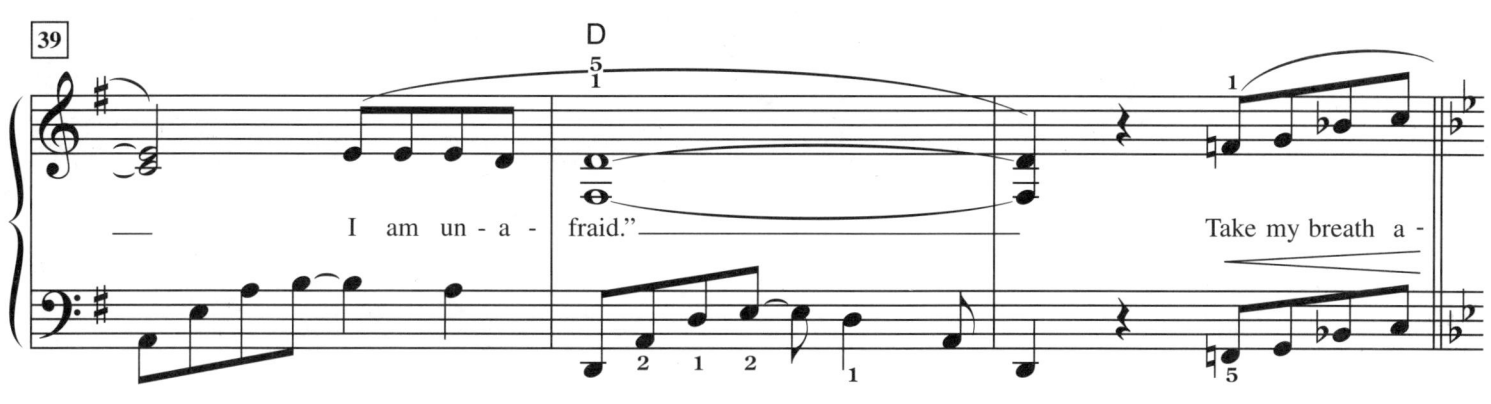

— I am un - a - fraid." Take my breath a -

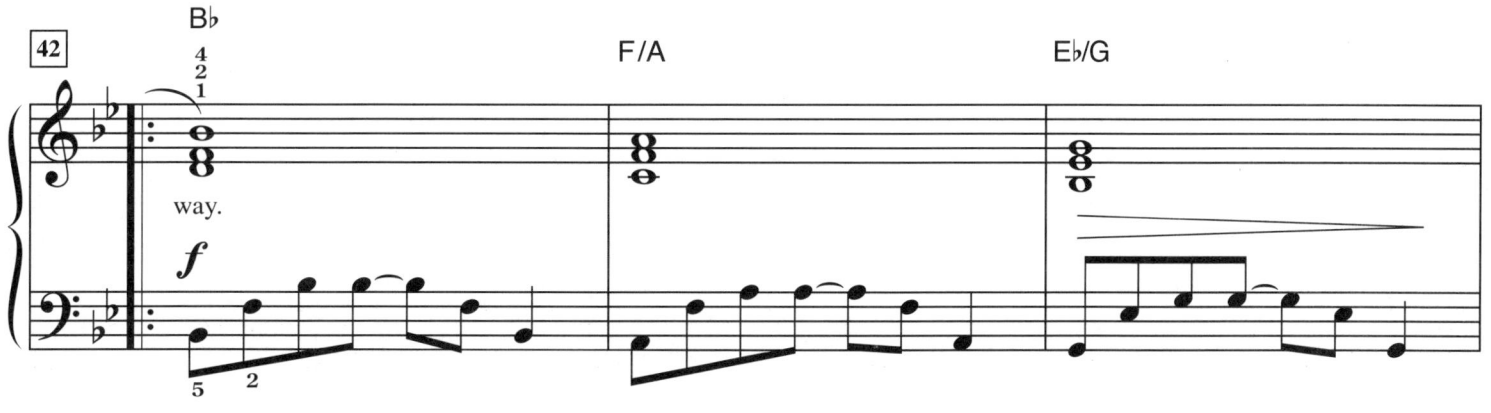

way.

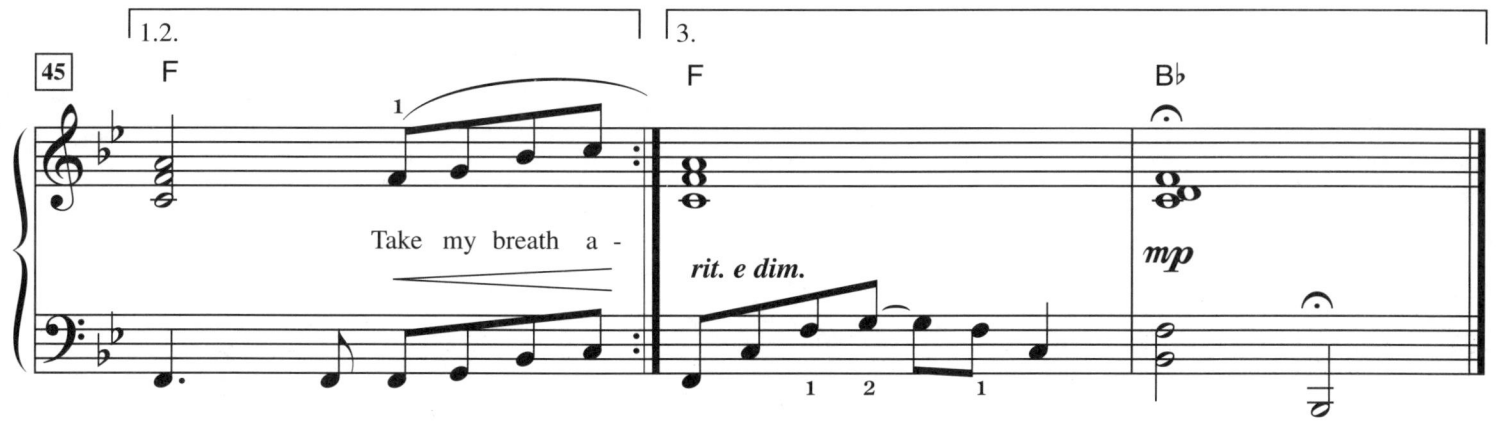

Take my breath a -

THE NOTEBOOK
(Main Title)

Written by Aaron Zigman
Arranged by Dan Coates

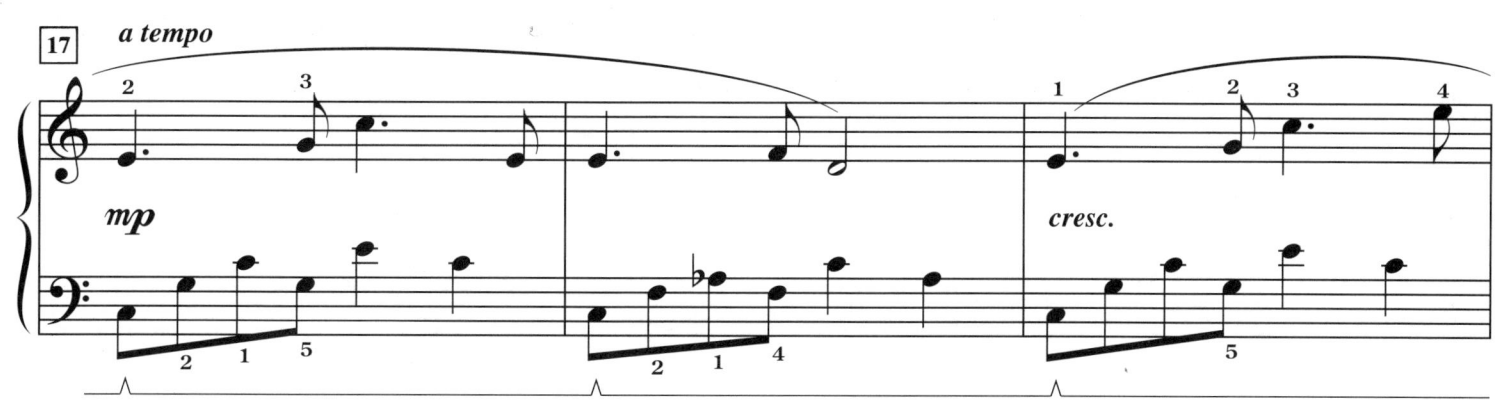

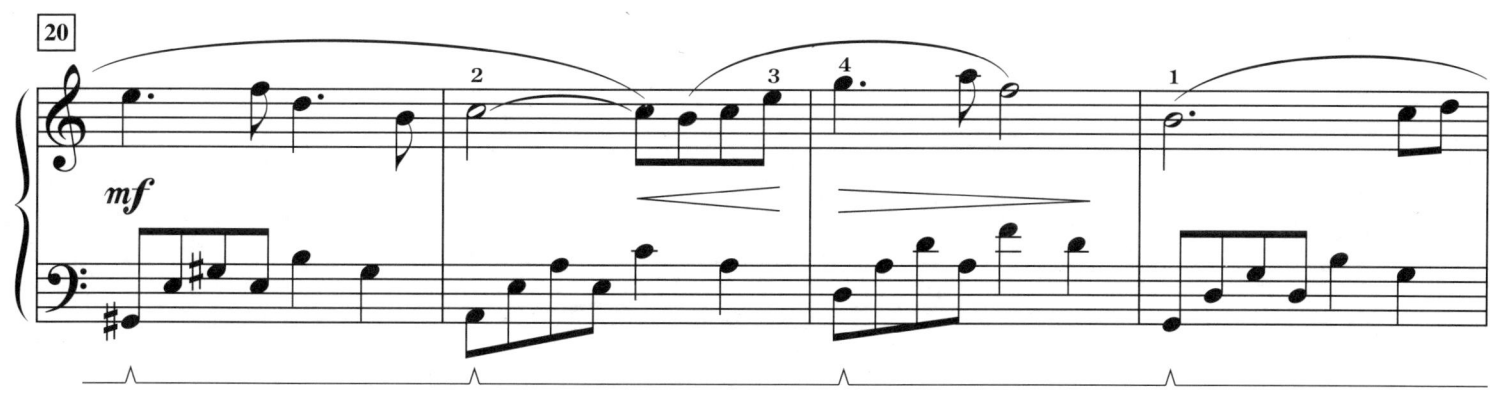

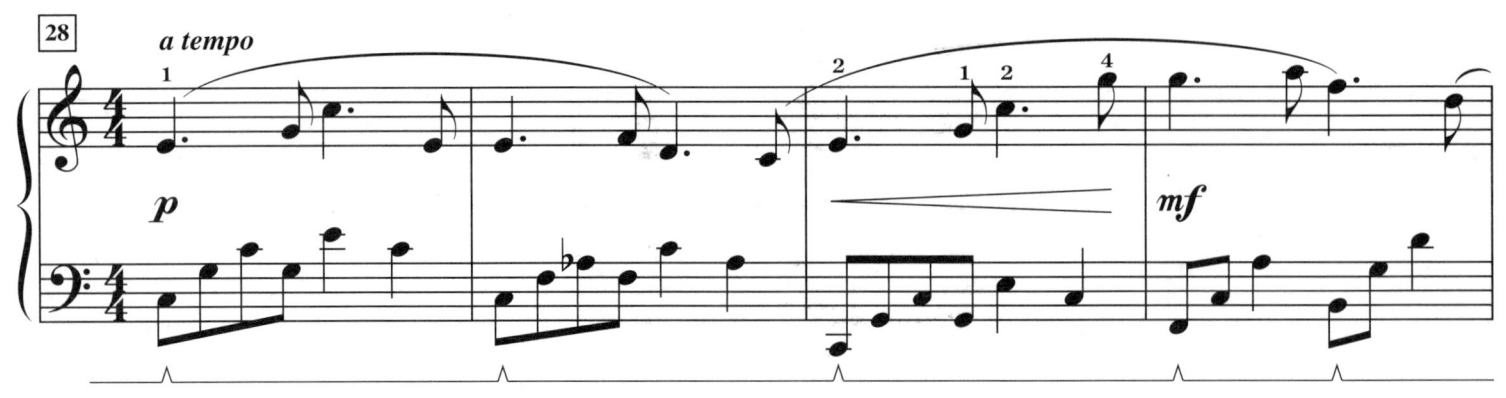

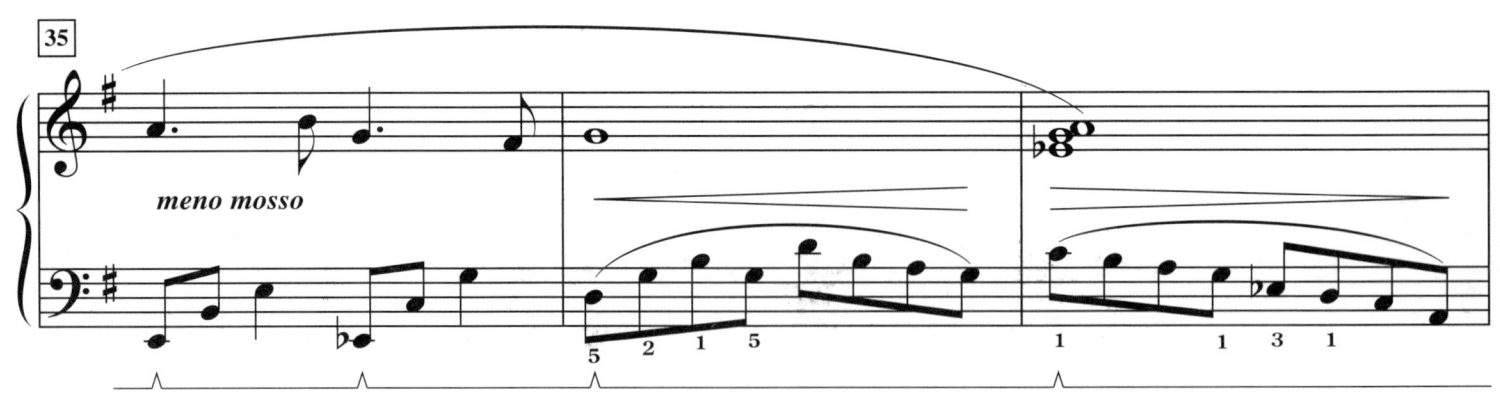